M

STALKING THE SOUL

STALKING THE SOUL

EMOTIONAL ABUSE AND THE

EROSION OF IDENTITY

MARIE-FRANCE HIRIGOYEN

AFTERWORD BY
THOMAS MOORE

*TRANSLATED FROM THE FRENCH
BY HELEN MARX*

HELEN MARX BOOKS

NEW YORK

M

Hirigoyen, Marie-France.
    [Le harcelement moral. English]
    Stalking the soul : emotional abuse and the erosion of identity /
Marie-France Hirigoyen ; translated from the French by Helen Marx. — 1st ed.
    p. cm.
    Includes bibliographical references.
    ISBN: 1-885586-53-1
    1. Psychological abuse.   2. Identity (Psychology).   3. Self-help.   I. Title.
RC569.5.P75H57   2000   616.85′82

CONTENTS

As there is no English equivalent to the gender-neutral French pronoun *on*, I have used gender-specific pronouns for descriptions of abusers and victims of abuse. Please note that these are arbitrary and interchangeable; abusers and victims can, of course, be either gender.

—H. M.

STALKING THE SOUL

A well-directed word
can kill or humiliate,
without dirtying one's hands.
One of the great joys in life
is humiliating one's equal.

—Pierre Desproges

What have I done to deserve such punishment?

There are, in life, stimulating encounters that encourage us to give our best; there are others that can undermine and ultimately destroy us. One individual can succeed in destroying another by a process of emotional abuse. This animosity sometimes culminates in a virtual murder of the soul. We have all witnessed emotionally abusive attacks in one form or another: in couples, in families, in the workplace, in social and political life. When faced with this indirect form of violence, our society puts on blinders. We acquiesce to the crime of emotional abuse under the guise of tolerance.

The evils of emotional abuse make excellent subject matter for movies (*Les Diaboliques* by Henri Georges Clouzot, 1954) or novels such as thrillers; public opinion, in these cases, clearly recognizes abusive manipulation, but back in our daily lives we hesitate to speak about it.

In the film *Tatie Danièle* by Etienne Chatiliez (1990), we are

3

amused at the emotional torment an old woman inflicts on those around her. She begins by torturing her old housekeeper to an "accidental" death. The spectator thinks, "She had it coming; she was too submissive!" Tatie Danièle next turns her wickedness on her nephew's family, who have taken her in. The nephew and his wife do all they can to make her life pleasant, but the more they do, the more vengeful she becomes.

Tatie Danièle uses a number of destabilizing techniques common to abusive people: innuendoes, spiteful allusions, lies, and humiliating remarks. We are astonished that the victims seem unaware of her manipulation. They try to understand her behavior and even feel responsible for it. "What have we done to make her hate us so much?" they wonder. Tatie Danièle doesn't throw tantrums; she is quiet, cold, and mean in a way that won't alert her entourage to what is happening. She uses small, unsettling touches that are difficult to spot. A woman of steel, Tatie Danièle turns the situation upside down by becoming the victim and making her family the persecutors: they are the ones who abandoned an eighty-two-year-old woman, leaving her in an apartment by herself with only dog food to eat.

In this supposedly humorous cinematic example, the victims don't react violently, a likely probability in real life; they hope their kindness will set an example and soften their aggressor. The opposite occurs because too much kindness becomes an unbearable provocation. The only person who finally finds favor in Tatie Danièle's eyes is a newcomer who operates on her level and ultimately brings her down. A quasi love relationship is introduced.

If this old woman amuses and moves us, it is because we feel that so much wickedness only springs from great suffering on her part. We pity her as her family does, and she ends up manipulating us just as she manipulates them. The poor victims seem so stupid that we withhold our pity. As Tatie Danièle becomes meaner, the family gets ever nicer, and both the audience and Tatie Danièle find them increasingly insufferable.

The fact remains that these are evil assaults. This aggression arises from an unconscious psychological process of destruction consisting of either hidden or overt hostility on the part of one and sometimes several abusers toward a designated person: a real target in every sense of the word. It is effectively possible to destabilize or even destroy someone with seemingly harmless words and hints, inferences, and unspoken suggestions; usually those close to the situation will not intervene. A narcissistic abuser grows in stature at the expense of the other; he also avoids any inner or spiritual conflict by shifting the responsibility for what is wrong onto the other person. If the other is responsible for the problem, wrong-doing, guilt, and suffering don't exist. This defines emotional abuse.

Every one of us can be guilty of this kind of wrong-doing, but the behavior only becomes destructive over time and through repetition. Any "normally neurotic" individual behaves abusively at certain times (in anger, for example), but he is also equally capable of other forms of behavior (hysterical, phobic, obsessive), and subsequently questions his abnormal actions. An abusive individual is, in a perverse way, always abusive; his relationship to "the other" is clearly and permanently defined and doesn't allow for uncertainty. Even if his abusiveness goes unnoticed for a period of time, it will manifest itself in situations where he becomes truly engaged and responsible. Self-doubt is unacceptable. In order to satisfy their insatiable need for admiration and approval, these individuals must degrade others to acquire first self-esteem and then power. Because they are not concerned with relationships, they show no compassion or respect for others. To respect another person is to value their humanity and acknowledge the suffering we can inflict upon them.

Perverse abusiveness fascinates, seduces, and terrifies. We sometimes envy abusive individuals because we imagine them endowed with a superior strength that will always make them winners. They do, in fact, know how to naturally manipulate, and this appears to give them the upper hand, whether in business or in politics. Fear makes us instinctively gravitate toward them rather than away from them: survival of the fittest. The most admired individuals are those who enjoy themselves the most and suffer the least. In any case, we don't take their victims, who seem weak and dense, seriously, and under the guise of respecting another's freedom, we become blind to potentially destructive situations. In fact, this tolerance prevents us from interfering in the actions and opinions of others, even when these actions and opinions seem out of line or morally reprehensible. We also weirdly indulge the lies and "spin" of those in power. The end justifies the means. To what degree is this acceptable? Don't we, out of indifference, risk becoming accomplices in this process by losing our principles and sense of limits? Real tolerance means examining and weighing values. This type of aggression, however, lays traps in the psychic domain of another person and is allowed to develop because of tolerance within our current socio-cultural context. Our era refuses to establish absolute standards of behavior. We automatically set limits on certain abusive behaviors when we label them as such; in our society this is likened with intent to censure. We have abandoned the moral and religious constraints that once constituted a code of civility which allowed us to say, "That just isn't done!" We only become indignant when facts are made public, worked over and magnified by the media.

Leaders no longer operate within a framework of conduct, but acquit themselves of their responsibilities by passing them on to the very same people they are supposed to guide or assist.

Even psychiatrists hesitate to use the term "abuse"; when they do, it's to express either their powerlessness to intervene or their fascination with the abuser's methods. The very definition of emotional abusiveness is challenged by some who prefer using the catch-all term of "psychopathy," under which they shelve anything they can't cure. Psychiatric illness does not cause abusiveness. It arises from dispassionate rationality combined with an incapacity to respect others as human beings. Some abusive people commit crimes for which they are judged, but most use charm and their adaptive powers to clear themselves a path in society, leaving behind a trail of wounded souls and devastated lives. Psychiatrists, attorneys, and educators—we have all been fooled by abusive human beings who passed themselves off as victims. They fulfilled our expectations in order the better to seduce us, thus confirming their neurotic feelings. We subsequently felt betrayed and humiliated when, in their search for power, they showed their true colors. This explains the reluctance of some psychiatrists to expose them. Psychiatrists say to each other, "Watch out, he's a perverse abuser," the implication being, "This could be dangerous," and also, "There's nothing that can be done." We then give up on helping the victims. Designating perversity is certainly a serious matter, one usually reserved for acts of great cruelty that are difficult even for psychiatrists to imagine—the crimes of serial killers, for example. Whether the subject is serial killing or perverse abusiveness, the matter remains one of predatory behavior: an act consisting in the appropriation of another person's life. The word "perverse" shocks and unsettles. It corresponds to a value judgment, and psychoanalysts refuse to pronounce

8 value judgments. Is that sufficient reason to accept what goes on? A more serious omission lies in not labeling abuse, because the victim then remains defenseless and vulnerable to attack.

In my clinical practice as a psychotherapist I have listened to cases of victims' suffering and their powerlessness to defend themselves. I subsequently will show that predators first paralyze their victims in order to prevent any possible counter-attack. The lack of defense mechanisms keeps victims from understanding what is happening to them. In order to help victims and future victims avoid the emotional snares of abusers, I will also try to analyze the process of abusive bonding which links the attacker to his or her prey.

Victims are often not heard when they seek help. Instead, analysts advise them to assess their conscious or unconscious responsibility for the attack upon them. Often psychoanalysis only considers the intrapsychic, or what goes on inside an individual's head, without assessing environmental impact. Analysis therefore ignores the issue of the victim as masochistic accomplice. And because of the aforementioned professional reticence in designating attacker and victim, therapists may even intensify the victim's destructive process. In my opinion, classic therapeutic methods are insufficient to help this type of victim. I shall recommend more suitable methods, specifically targeting emotional aggression and abuse.

The intent is not to put emotional abusers on trial—they are more than capable of defending themselves—but to bear in mind the injury and peril they can inflict; remembering this fact will help victims and future victims defend themselves. Even when, and justly so, this form of aggression is viewed as a defense mechanism (against psychosis or depression), this cannot exonerate emotional abusers. There are fairly innocuous manipulative tricks that leave behind traces of bitterness or shame at having been duped, but there are much more serious manipulations that affect a victim's core identity and become a matter of life or death. Emotional abusers directly endanger their victims; indirectly, they lead those around them to lose sight of their moral guideposts and to believe that freewheeling behaviors at the expense of others are the norm.

As a victimologist, I shall not undertake in this book a theoretical discussion on the nature of abuse, but will squarely side with the victims of abuse. Victimology, a fairly recent branch of psychology, was originally a branch of criminology. It analyzes the causes and process of victimization, its consequences, and the rights of the victim. A degree in victimology can be of particular interest to professionals in the field of helping victims: emergency-trained doctors, psychiatrists, psychotherapists, and lawyers.

A person who has undergone psychic aggression such as emotional abuse is truly a victim because his or her psyche has been, to a greater or lesser degree, permanently altered. Even if a victim's reactions to emotional abuse contribute to a sustained, even seemingly equal, relationship with the aggressor, one must not forget that this person suffers from a situation for which he or she is not responsible. When victims of this insidious form of violence do consult a psychotherapist, it is generally for the treatment of a self-contained problem such as mental inhibition and lack of confidence or assertiveness; it can also be a state of permanent depression that is unresponsive to medication, or a more intense depression potentially leading to suicide. If they sometimes complain about their "partner" or those around them, they also seem unaware of the terrible subterranean violence that threatens them. This pre-existing state of psychic confusion can make even the psychotherapist gloss over the question of objective violence. These situations share a common unthinkable element: the victims, while recognizing their suffering, cannot really imagine that violence and abuse have taken place. Sometimes doubt persists: "Am I making it all up, as others have suggested?" When and if they dare to complain about what is happening, they feel inadequate to describe it and therefore assume they are misunderstood.

I have deliberately chosen the terms "perverse abuser" and "victim" because this is a case of hidden but authentic violence.

PART I

EMOTIONAL
ABUSE

CHAPTER ONE

EMOTIONAL ABUSE IN PRIVATE LIFE

S mall acts of abuse are so common in daily life that they appear normal. The process begins with a lack of respect, a lie, or a simple manipulative act. We find it unacceptable only when we are affected. If the social group in which this behavior arises fails to react, the behavior evolves progressively to the next stage: distinctly abusive conduct with serious consequences for the psychological health of its victims. Not sure of being understood, victims of abuse keep quiet and suffer in silence.

This kind of moral destruction has always existed: in families, where it usually remains hidden, and in a business framework, where people put up with it during periods of full employment because, after all, the victims are free to resign at any time. In periods of unemployment, they cling desperately to their jobs, thereby injuring their physical and psychical health. Some have fought back and sued. Today, society has begun to ask questions as this phenomenon becomes more publicized.

Psychotherapeutic practitioners are frequently witness to

14   life stories where the boundaries between outside, or environmental, and psychological realities blur. The commonality of suffering in these stories is striking: the experience each person believes to be unique is shared by many others.

The difficulty of clinical transcriptions lies in weighing the importance of every word, every intonation, and every allusion. The details, taken separately, seem harmless, but added together, they show a destructive process. The victim is swept along in this deadly game and will sometimes resort to an abusive mode of behavior because this kind of defense tactic can be used by anyone. This line of conduct can lead to wrongfully accusing the victim of becoming an accomplice to the abuser.

I have seen, in the course of my clinical practice, how the same abusive individuals tend to replicate destructive conduct in all areas of life: at work, in their marriage, with their children. It is this behavioral continuity that I would like to emphasize. There are individuals whose road through life is strewn with people they have wounded or irreparably damaged. This doesn't prevent them from fooling most people and from seeming to be totally adjusted social beings.

EMOTIONAL ABUSE IN COUPLES

Emotional abuse in couples is often denied or made light of by reducing it to a simple question of dominance. A psychoanalytical simplification of the phenomenon would consist in representing the partner as an accomplice to, or even responsible for, the abusive relationship. This denies the dimension of control in the equation that paralyzes the victim and prevents him or her from self-defense; it also denies the violence of these attacks and the far-reaching psychological consequences of abuse. Because the aggression is so subtle, leaving no tangible traces, witnesses tend to interpret as simple conflicts or "love-spats" what are in fact attempts to morally or even physically destroy another person. These efforts are sometimes successful.

I shall describe several couples at different stages in the evolution of emotional abuse. The unequal length of my case histories is due to the fact that this process takes place over a period of months, even years: as abusive relationships evolve, the victims first learn to mentally register what occurs, and later learn how to defend themselves and gather proof as evidence.

CONTROL

The impulse to emotionally abuse is set in motion when the "loved one" is somehow found lacking or the relationship is too symbiotic.

The most intimate other will become the subject of the greatest abuse because too much closeness can terrify the aggressor. A narcissistic individual imposes control on his partner in order to hold her back, while simultaneously fearing her closeness and invasiveness. In order to maintain complete power over her, she must be kept in a dependent or even proprietary relationship. The partner mired in doubt and guilt cannot react.

The unspoken message is "I don't love you," but it remains indirect and hidden so the other won't leave. The partner must stay put and be permanently frustrated; she must be prevented from thinking on her own and becoming aware of the process. In an interview, writer Patricia Highsmith describes it as follows: "Sometimes the people who attract us the most, or whom we love the most, spark our imagination as effectively as insulators on rubber."

16   The narcissistic abuser introduces the element of control to paralyze his partner by putting her in a situation of flux and uncertainty. Keeping her within limits and at a safe distance avoids commitment to a relationship he fears. By stifling and subjugating her, he forces her to submit to what he most dreads and must at all costs avoid: invasiveness by another person. Within normally functioning couples, even where elements of control exist, there should be a dynamic of mutually narcissistic reinforcement. There are cases where an individual seeks to theoretically extinguish his partner, thereby consolidating his dominant position. But in couples ruled by an abusive narcissist the relationship can be literally deadly: vilification and underhanded attacks are routine and systematic.

The too-tolerant partner makes this process possible. Such tolerance is often interpreted by psychoanalysts as being linked to the basically unconscious masochistic benefits that can be gained from the relationship. We shall see that this interpretation is only partial because in most cases the parties had previously shown no self-punishment tendencies, nor did such tendencies show up later. An incomplete analysis is dangerous because reinforcing the party's guilt completely prevents him or her from finding ways to escape the constricted situation.

The sources of this tolerance are most often found in a feeling of family loyalty that consists, for example, in reliving a parent's experience or in accepting the sacrificial role of compensating for the other's narcissism.

Benjamin and Annie met two years ago. Annie was then in a frustrating relationship with a married man. Benjamin is jealous of this man. He is in love with Annie and begs her to break off the affair: he wants to marry her and have children. Annie breaks off easily and although she keeps her own apartment, she basically lives with Benjamin.

Benjamin now begins to change. He becomes distant and indifferent, tender only when he wants sex. Annie demands explanations but Benjamin denies any behavioral change. Not liking confrontation, she tries to seem upbeat. When she is irritable, he doesn't seem to understand or react.

Little by little she becomes depressed. Since the relationship doesn't improve and Annie is still stunned by Benjamin's rejection, he finally realizes that something has happened; he simply couldn't bear to see her depressed. She begins therapy to treat her depression, ostensibly the cause of their problems.

Annie and Benjamin are in the same business. She has much more experience. He often asks her advice but refuses to accept any criticism. "It's no use, I've had enough, I don't know what you're talking about!" Several times he's appropriated her ideas, while denying the fact that her knowledge has helped him. He never thanks her.

He blames the mistakes she notices on his secretary. She pretends to believe him in order to avoid a scene.

He shrouds his work schedule and life under a veil of secrecy. She learns by chance of Benjamin's promotion from friends congratulating him. He lies all the time, saying he's coming back from a business trip on such and such a train when the ticket he leaves lying around reads otherwise.

In public, he remains very distant. At a cocktail party one time, he comes toward her and shakes her hand, saying: "Mademoiselle X, who's in such and such a business," then turns on his heel and walks off, leaving her alone. When she later asks for explanations, he mumbles something about being too busy.

Even though she earns her own living, he objects to her spending money and doesn't want her to buy clothes. He makes her line her shoes up in a row like a little girl. He teases her in public about her jars of makeup in the bathroom: "I don't know why you need to put all that stuff on your face!"

Annie asks herself how she can show affection to a man who judges her in everything: her gestures, her words, her spending. He refuses to discuss their relationship, saying, "The word 'relationship' is old hat." He won't engage with her. A clown stops them in the street one day to show them a magic trick, and says to Benjamin, "Your wife, right?" Benjamin doesn't answer and tries to move on. Annie takes it to mean, "He couldn't answer because the subject is unthinkable. I'm not his wife, his fiancée, or his girlfriend. The subject is taboo because it's too oppressive." Whenever she wants to talk about "them," he says, "Do you really think this is the moment to bring that up?"

Other subjects, like her desire for a child, are equally hurtful. When they see friends with children, she tries not to seem overly enthusiastic because it might make Benjamin think she wants a child. She acts neutral, as if it were unimportant.

Benjamin wants to control Annie. He wants her to be financially independent but submissive at the same time; if not, he agonizes and rejects her.

When she talks at dinner, he rolls his eyes. At first she says to herself, "What I just said must be idiotic!" and then she begins to progressively censor herself.

However, from the onset of therapy, even if it causes tension, she does not accept a priori criticism from him.

There are no discussions between them, only arguments when she's had enough, like the straw that breaks the camel's back. In these cases, she's the only one to become angry. Benjamin looks surprised and says, "You're accusing me again. Naturally, for you, everything is my fault." She tries to explain: "I'm not saying it's your fault, I just want to talk about what's wrong!" He pretends not to understand and always succeeds in making her doubt herself and take the blame. Asking what's not working between them is like saying, "It's your fault." He doesn't want to hear, and ends the discussion or tries to slither out before she's even begun.

"I wish he'd say what he dislikes about me," Annie reasons. "Then, at least, we could have a discussion."

Little by little, they stop discussing politics because when she argues her points, he complains she isn't on his side. They also stop talking about Annie's business successes. Benjamin can't stand being in anyone's shadow. She's consciously aware of giving up her opinions and her individuality in order to keep the situation from going from bad to worse. This awareness motivates her to constantly try and make daily living bearable.

Sometimes she reacts and threatens to leave. He holds her back with double talk. "I want our relationship to continue . . . I can't give you more right now." She is so crazy about him that she takes hope at the slightest sign of their drawing closer.

Annie knows the relationship is abnormal but, having lost all benchmarks, she feels obliged to protect Benjamin and excuse him no matter what. She also knows he won't change, taking the attitude that "either I adapt or I leave." Their sex life is no better because Benjamin doesn't feel like making love anymore. She sometimes raises the subject:

"We can't go on living like this."

"That's the way it is, I can't make love on demand."

"What can we do? What can *I* do?"

"There isn't a solution for everything. You want to regulate it all!"

When she draws near to give him a loving hug, he licks her nose. If she objects, he accuses her of definitely lacking a sense of humor.

What keeps Annie with him?

It would be simpler if Benjamin were an absolute monster, but he was once a tender lover. He acts like this because he's not well. He can change. She will therefore change him. She watches for the change. She hopes one day a thread will unwind and they'll finally be able to communicate.

She feels responsible for the change in Benjamin: He couldn't bear to see her depressed. She feels equally guilty for not being seductive enough (he had joked one time in front of friends about an unsexy outfit Annie was wearing) and for not being good enough to gratify Benjamin (he had alluded to the fact that she wasn't generous).

She tells herself that staying with Benjamin in an unsatisfying relationship is better than being alone. Benjamin once said to her, "If we separate I'll find someone right away but you, with your desire for being alone, will stay all alone." And she believes him. Even though she recognizes that she's more sociable than Benjamin, she imagines that alone and regretful, she'll be depressed.

She realizes, too, that her parents stayed together out of duty and have an unhappy marriage. There had always been violence at home, but because it was a family where things remained unsaid, the violence was insidious.

VIOLENCE

Abusive violence appears in times of crisis when an individual with abusive defenses cannot assume responsibility for a difficult decision. The violence then becomes indirect, essentially as a form of disrespect for the other.

Monique and Luke have been married for thirty years. Luke has been having an affair for six months. He announces this to Monique, adding that he can't choose between the two women. He wants to stay married and continue the affair. Monique adamantly refuses. Her husband leaves.

Monique has been a complete wreck ever since. She cries all the time; she doesn't sleep and doesn't eat. She shows psychosomatic symptoms of anxiety: cold sweats, stomachaches, tachycardia. She is angry not at her husband, who makes her suffer, but at herself, for not being able to keep him. It would be easier for Monique to protect herself if she could feel anger toward her husband. But to feel anger, one must see the other as aggressive and violent, which would result in not wanting his return. It's easier when one is in a state of shock like Monique to deny the reality of the facts and to wait, even if waiting means suffering.

Luke asks Monique to see him regularly in order to maintain their bond; if she doesn't agree, he might leave forever. On the other hand, if she withdraws from him, he will forget her. When she acts depressed, he doesn't want to be with her. He even suggests to Monique, on the advice of his analyst, that she meet his friend so "word will get around."

He doesn't seem for a minute to have thought about his wife's suffering. He simply states that he's sick of her lifeless behavior. By blaming his wife for not being able to stay with him, he avoids taking responsibility for the separation.

Refusing responsibility for marital failure is often the cause of setting abuse in motion. An individual with idealistic ideas about marriage carries on an apparently normal relationship with his partner until the day he has to choose between this relationship and a new one. Abuse will grow in proportion to yesterday's idealism. It is impossible to entirely accept responsibility for a failure of this kind. The partner is held responsible when love is withdrawn because she has committed an unnamed fault. The denial of love is acted upon although often verbally denied.

Recognizing this manipulative behavior leaves the victim in a state of terrible anxiety she cannot get rid of alone. At this stage, victims experience shame as well as anger: shame at not being loved, shame at having accepted humiliation, and shame at what they have submitted to and undergone.

In some cases, it is a question not of becoming abusive, but of manifesting a previously hidden emotionally abusive nature. This overt hate, now revealed, resembles a persecution complex. Role reversal takes place: the aggressor becomes the victimized one, although the real victim still feels the guilt. To make the situation credible, the other must be forced to behave unacceptably so that she can then be invalidated.

Both architects, Anna and Paul meet at work. Paul quickly decides to move in with Anna but keeps his distance emotionally and avoids commitment. He shuns terms of endearment and affectionate gestures in public, and makes fun of couples holding hands.

Paul has difficulty expressing anything personal. He appears to joke non-stop, making fun of everything. This strategy allows him to hide and to remain uninvolved. He is also a real misogynist. His attitude is "We can't live without them, but women are castrating, frivolous, and insufferable."

Anna interprets Paul's coldness as reserve, his rigidity as strength, and his innuendoes as knowledge. She believes that her love and the reassurance of their relationship will make him less hard.

They establish an implicit rule of little or no open intimacy. Anna accepts and justifies this rule, thereby legitimizing it. Because she wants a close relationship more than Paul does, it is up to her to make the necessary moves that will allow it to continue. Paul explains his hardness as resulting from a difficult childhood, but there's an air of mystery to the contradictory and partial information he provides: "Nobody took care of me when I was little. If my grandmother hadn't been there for me . . ." "My father may not even be my real father."

Posing as a victim from the beginning, he makes Anna feel sorry for him and be more indulgent and caring than she might ordinarily. Because of her healing instincts, Anna is quickly seduced by this hurt little boy.

One of those people who "just know," Paul has radical opinions on every subject: politics, the future, who's foolish and who's not, how to act and how not to act. Most of the time, he conveys his infinite wisdom with a simple nod of the head or an unfinished sentence. He very skillfully provides a mirror for Anna's insecurities.

Anna is a doubter. Unsure of herself, she doesn't judge others but finds extenuating circumstances as reasons for their behavior. She always tries to shade her opinions, a habit that Paul calls "complicating your life." Little by little, Anna softens her harshness in front of Paul in order to conform to his expectations or to what she believes they might be. She tries not to be too insistent about things and tries to change her habits.

Their relationship is based on a pattern of "he knows—she doubts." She finds it relaxing to depend on another person's certainties. He senses her compliance and readiness to accept his pronouncements.

Paul, from the start of their relationship, has always been extremely critical of Anna. He attacks with small, unsettling jabs, preferably in public, where it's difficult for her to react. When she tries to talk about it later, he coldly says that she bears grudges and makes mountains out of molehills. It usually starts with a fairly harmless but intimate fact that Paul, occasionally picking an ally from the group, exaggerates: "Don't you think Anna listens to music that's 'old hat'?" "I bet you didn't know she buys expensive creams to firm up her practically non-existent breasts." "She doesn't understand *that*, when any dodo can."

When they're going away with friends for the weekend, he'll point to Anna's bag, saying, "She thinks I'm a moving man. Why not take the bathtub?" If Anna protests with "What do you care? I'm carrying it myself!" Paul answers, "Sure, but if you're tired, I'll have to carry it or look like a boor. You don't need two changes of clothes and three tubes of lipstick."

Then he generalizes about female duplicity, which ultimately forces men to help out.

Embarrassing Anna is what really matters. She senses the hostility but isn't quite sure about her instincts because it's all said in such a bittersweet, half-joking way. The hostility isn't necessarily picked up on by the group, and Anna can't react without seeming humorless.

When someone has complimented Anna and she seems to have the upper hand, Paul is even more critical. Then she realizes that he's a bundle of complexes when it comes to her natural ease with people and her greater business success and earning power. After criticizing her, he will add, "That's not a reproach, it's a fact."

The emotional abuse appears when Paul decides to settle in with a young associate. His strategic ploys to destabilize Anna become more overt.

The first manifestation of abuse is a permanent bad mood, which Paul attributes to business and money problems. He arrives home before Anna most evenings, and settles down with a drink in front of the television set. When Anna comes in, he doesn't answer her greeting but asks, without turning his head, "What are we eating?" (a classic strategy to transfer one's bad mood onto the other person).

He never reproaches her directly. Instead, he'll casually toss out some seemingly innocuous remark in a hurt tone of voice that she'll have to think about later. If Anna tries to clarify what he said, he slithers out of it and denies any aggressiveness on his part.

He starts calling her "old bag." When she objects, he changes the nickname to "fat old bag," saying, "You don't have to take it personally, since you're not fat!"

When she tries to explain how she suffers, it's as though she faces a blank wall. He gets stony and she persists, which makes him even harder. Invariably, she ends up losing her temper, and Paul can then point out that she's an aggressive shrew. She never steps back far enough to understand or diffuse the violence.

Unlike in most marital scenes, they don't really fight, which makes reconciliation impossible. Paul never raises his voice; he only displays an icy hostility that he subsequently denies if the matter is brought up. Frustrated by the lack of dialogue, Anna loses her temper and yells. Then he mocks her anger with "Calm down, poor baby!" and she feels ridiculous.

Looks communicate the essence of their relationships: looks of hate from Paul and looks of reproach and fear from Anna.

The only concrete fact is Paul's refusal to have sex. When she wants to discuss this, it's never the right moment. He's exhausted at night, rushed in the morning, and has things to do during the day. She decides to pin him down in a restaurant. Once there, she begins to talk about her hurt. Paul immediately interrupts her in a tone of icy fury: "I hope you're not going to make a scene in the restaurant, particularly about a subject like that. You really are completely out of control!"

Paul is beside himself when Anna starts to cry. "You are depressed and angry all the time," he tells her.

Later, Paul justifies himself another way: "How can I make love to you? You're a horror, and a castrating witch!"

Some time after that, he goes so far as to steal a business agenda she uses for her accounting records. Anna looks for it and asks Paul if he has seen the book. No one else has been in the room where she is certain she left it. Paul answers that he hasn't seen it and that, furthermore, she should be neater. His look is so full of hatred that she is thunderstruck with fear. She realizes he has stolen it, but is too frightened by the violence that might erupt if she persists.

The worst of it is that she doesn't understand. She searches for reasons: Does he want to hurt her directly, knowing the trouble this would cause her? Is it jealousy? A need to verify that she works harder than he does? Or does he hope to find a mistake in the agenda that he can use against her?

She does recognize, without a doubt, that the act is malicious. It's such a terrible thought that she chases it away, refusing to believe it; her fear becomes physical anxiety whenever Paul looks at her in the same hateful way.

Anna feels very clearly at this stage that Paul wants to utterly destroy her identity.

Instead of putting small doses of arsenic in her coffee, as they do in English murder mysteries, he is trying to break her psychologically.

He has objectified Anna in order not to be affected by her suffering. He looks at her coldly, unemotionally; seen in that way, her tears do seem ridiculous. What Anna feels most deeply, however, is that she doesn't exist for Paul. Her tears and suffering remain unheard, or, more precisely, it's as if they don't exist. The complete breakdown of communication between them unleashes terrible anger in Anna and, because it can't be vented, turns into anxiety.

She then tries to tell him that a separation is preferable to this daily torture, but it's impossible to raise the subject during a crisis when whatever she might say will be ignored. When life is bearable, periodically, she holds her breath so as not to create additional tension.

Anna tries writing to Paul, explaining how she suffers and only wants to find a solution to their situation. She puts the first letter on Paul's desk and waits for him to say something. Since he doesn't mention it, she dares to ask what he thinks. He answers coldly, "I have nothing to say on the subject." Anna tells herself she wasn't clear enough. She writes a longer letter that she finds in the wastebasket the next day. Frantically, she demands an explanation. He dismisses her by saying he doesn't have to acknowledge her overwrought claims.

Whatever she does simply doesn't make a difference. Is it the way she puts things? From then on, she photocopies her letters to him.

Paul remains impervious to Anna's suffering because he doesn't even see it. This is intolerable for Anna who, in her anguish, acts even clumsier. The violence on his part is justified because he perceives her mistakes as character flaws that should be corrected. She has become too dangerous for him and, therefore, must be "broken."

Paul's reaction to this reciprocal violence is an avoidance of it, while Anna's is a predictable attempt to communicate. She decides to separate from Paul.

Paul says, "If I understand correctly, you're throwing me out without a penny!"

"I'm not throwing you out. I just can't stand the situation any longer. You have money. You work like I do, and when we reach a settlement, you'll take half."

"Where will I go? You're really nasty. Because of you, I'll have to live in a slum."

Anna blames herself for Paul's violent reaction, excusing it because of his enforced separation from the children.

After his first weekend with them, Anna runs into them all on the street on their way home. They tell her they've had a nice day with Sheila, their father's associate. In that instant she sees a triumphant smirk on Paul's face that she doesn't immediately comprehend.

Once home, the children can't wait to tell her how in love Daddy is. He spent the entire day kissing Sheila on the mouth, and touching her breasts and behind. Lacking the courage to tell Anna directly that he has a girlfriend, he sends messages indirectly via his children. He knows his intimacy with Sheila will make Anna jealous, but far from home he won't even have to hear or fear Anna's legitimate reproaches. By placing his children front and center to absorb their mother's bitterness and sadness, he shows no respect for either the mother or the children.

Anna is out of her depth. The more she struggles, the deeper she sinks. Afraid to make a move and unable to say or do anything, she swings between anguish and rage. She can no longer fight, and lets herself founder and be swallowed up by her intense pain.

Paul lets his family and friends know that Anna threw him out of the house and how difficult financially that is for him. Refusing to act the role of villain he has cast her in, Anna tries to justify herself by using a method that didn't work even when they were together: writing to Paul and explaining her feelings. Too frightened to attack Paul directly, she blames his mistress, Sheila, for seducing a vulnerable married man.

She falls into Paul's trap by doing this. He wants to stay above anger and hate. He dodges the situation and puts the two women head-to-head. Anna, still meek and protective, will not confront Paul.

She only once dares to attack him directly. She goes to his apartment, enters forcibly, and says everything she's been holding back all this time. It's their only real "scene from a marriage," and her only real confrontation with Paul. "You're crazy, and one doesn't talk to crazy people," he tells her. When he tries to push her out the door, she slaps him and leaves, crying. Naturally, Paul immediately uses this scene against Anna. She gets a summons from his lawyer. Paul spreads the word that Anna is crazy and violent. Paul's mother reproaches her: "Really, Anna dear, you must calm yourself; your behavior is unacceptable!"

Anna and Paul's lawyers negotiate a settlement. Anna picks a lawyer with a non-confrontational reputation, because she wants above all to keep Paul calm and avoid a prolonged negotiation. Anna wants to be conciliatory and she doesn't argue, which makes her seem all-powerful and even more menacing.

Although they had agreed to do an inventory of their possessions, Anna learns just by chance before a vacation that Paul has emptied out the country house. He left only the children's beds and some of Anna's family's furniture. Anna resigns herself, thinking that once the finances are settled, Paul will stop attacking her, but it doesn't work that way.

She hears about remarks Paul has made questioning her integrity. At first she tries to defend herself, explaining that everything has been handled by lawyers, then suddenly sees there's no point to it because she has to be guilty of something. One day one of the children says to her, "Papa tells everyone you took everything from him. Maybe it's true. How do we know you're not dishonest?"

In this example, we see that Paul cannot assume responsibility for the break-up. He sets the scene so that Anna will be forced to take the initiative and throw him out. She thereby becomes responsible for the couple's split. She is to blame for the whole situation and she is the scapegoat who keeps Paul from any self-doubt. If Anna had reacted violently to this betrayal, she would have been labeled violent. But she collapses and is called crazy and depressed. She is wrong in any case. Because her reactions aren't excessive, she can only be invalidated by slander and insinuation.

Anna must learn to accept that no matter what she does, Paul will always hate her, and that nothing will change the relationship. She is powerless and must therefore build a strong enough self-image so that Paul's abuse will not erode her identity. She will then stop being terrified of her abuser, and will cut off his aggressiveness by being out of the game.

For Paul, it's as though in order to love one person, he has to hate another. We all have a suicidal strain, and a way of ridding oneself of it is to project this death wish outwardly onto someone else. That is why certain individuals divide people into "good" and "bad." It doesn't pay to be in the bad-guy camp.

An abuser needs to turn his previous partner into a scapegoat and project everything bad onto her in order to idealize the new love object and establish a relationship. Any obstacle

30 standing in the way has to be destroyed. For love to exist, there must be hate somewhere. The new relationship is founded on hatred of the previous partner.

This process is common in separations, but more often than not the hatred subsides, as does the idealization of the new partner. Because Paul deeply idealizes marriage and the family, the process is heightened in order to protect his new family. Sheila, consciously or not, feels that this hate protects her relationship with Paul, and doesn't try to put a stop to it. On one level, she may even activate this protective phenomenon.

Anna, naturally naive, thinks that being in love makes one generous, happy, and "a better person." She doesn't understand that Paul loves someone else. She thinks that if Paul rejects her, it's because she's "not good enough" to live up to his expectations. On the contrary, with abusive individuals, love must be split off and surrounded by hate.

SEPARATION

Abusive methods are common in divorce or separation and are not initially considered pathological. During separations, previously buried abusive impulses surface to unleash a cunning violence that takes over when the abusive narcissist feels his prey escaping.

The violence remains uninterrupted during the separation and continues via the remaining links between the couple, including children. According to J. G. Lemaire, "Vindictive conduct, after separation or divorce, can be understood in this framework: a person, in order not to hate himself, needs to find an outlet for all his hatred in an individual who has once been a part of him."[1]

This is called *stalking*, or harassment. Harassment or stalking exists when old lovers or partners don't want to let go of their prey and encroach on their ex-partners' identity and soul with their presence: waiting for them after work, telephoning them day and night, menacing them directly or indirectly.

Stalking is taken seriously in many states, which provide protective orders, because it has been established that this behavior can easily lead to physical violence if the victim reacts.

No matter who initiates the separation, divorce with abusive narcissists is violent and litigious. These procedures continue to refer to "the couple," which essentially doesn't exist anymore. The stronger the impulse to control, the greater the resentment and the anger. The victims defend themselves badly, particularly if they have initiated the break (as is often the case); their guilt inclines them to be generous, and they hope this will result in escape from their persecutor.

Whereas victims rarely know how to use the law in their favor, the aggressor instinctively deploys the necessary maneuvers. Abusive behavior can be used to find fault in a divorce action. But how can one keep track of guilt by innuendo? The plaintiff must prove his action with facts. How can one prove abusive schemes?

It's not unusual for the abusive partner, having forced his spouse into action, to pounce on this lack of proof and use it to his advantage. Judges, fearing that they themselves will be manipulated, and not knowing who manipulates whom in a relationship, will play it safe and remain uncommitted.

The goal of abusive conduct is to destabilize the other person and make them doubt themselves and others. Anything goes in order to achieve this end: lies, improbabilities, innuendoes. The spouse, in order not to be intimidated, must not yield to self-doubt or question her decisions and must ignore the abuse. This obliges her to be alert at all times when in contact with her ex-spouse.

Elaine and Pierre separate after ten years of marriage and three chil-dren. Elaine complains of her husband's violence and asks for the divorce. In front of the judge, Pierre predicts what will happen in the years to come: "From now on, my only aim in life will be to make Elaine's life miserable."

He thereafter refuses all direct communication with her; ex-changes are made by registered mail or through their lawyers. If he happens to get her on the telephone when calling the children, he simply says, "Put the children on!" If they happen to meet on the street, not only does he not answer her hello, but looks right through her as if she were invisible. By not looking at her, he makes her feel, without words, that she doesn't exist, that she is nothing.

As is often the case with divorced couples like this, insidious ha-rassment begins with negotiations about the children: their vaca-tions, health, and school. Every letter from Pierre is a seemingly harmless but nonetheless unsettling small act of emotional abuse.

He responds to a letter from Elaine about a new school lunch pro-gram with: "Given your usual dishonesty, at least let me discuss this with my lawyer." When she sends a registered letter (because other-wise he won't answer), he remarks, "One has to be crazy or dishonest to send a registered letter every eight days."

To a letter asking him about the allocation of weekends in May, he says, "The weekend of the 7th and 8th is the first weekend of the month. In view of what's happened in the past, my lawyer recom-mends that I formally notify you that I will file complaint if you don't respect the proper dates."

These letters invariably make Elaine ask, "What have I done?" Even when she thinks she hasn't done anything, she wonders if maybe she has overlooked a fact that Pierre has misinterpreted. She justifies herself at first, but then realizes that the more she does it, the guiltier she appears.

Elaine reacts violently to all this indirect aggression, and because Pierre is out of harm's way, it is the children who see her crying and screaming like a madwoman.

Elaine would like to be irreproachable, but in Pierre's eyes, she is guilty of everything—no matter what. She has become a scapegoat: responsible for the separation and its consequences. Her attempts at justification are pitiful and useless.

It is impossible for Elaine to defend herself against Pierre's insinuations since she has no idea what he is referring to. Justification is impossible. She is guilty of something they don't name but are both supposed to know. If she discusses these malicious exchanges with her family and friends, they make light of them by saying, "He'll calm down; it's not serious."

Pierre refuses to communicate directly with Elaine. When she writes to warn him about an important matter with the children, he doesn't answer. If she calls, he either says, "I don't wish to speak to you," and hangs up, or hurts her with a cold tone of voice. On the other hand, if she does make a decision without informing him, he immediately lets her know through his lawyer or by mail that he disagrees; he then puts pressure on the children to have the action fail. In this way, Pierre paralyzes Elaine from making decisions about the children. Not content with showing she's a bad wife, he also has to show she's a bad mother. He doesn't care that his behavior will also destabilize his children.

When faced with any important decision concerning the children, Elaine agonizes about asking for Pierre's advice without creating an argument, and then finally sends a letter in which every word is carefully measured. He doesn't answer. She acts unilaterally. A registered letter follows: "Your decision was set in motion without my foreknowledge or advice. May I remind you that I share parental authority with you over our three children and that, consequently, you cannot make a decision without consulting me." The same speech is addressed to the children, who no longer know who decides for them.

A few years after their separation, she has to decide something important for one of the children. She writes, but as usual, there's no answer. She calls. She knows right away that nothing has changed.

"You read my letter; do you agree?" she asks.

"There's nothing one can do with a mother like you, no use even trying because it'll just happen the way you want. You always do what you want and so do the children. Anyway, you're far from perfect. You are a thief and a liar who spends her time hurting people. That's all that interests you and that's all you do."

"I'm not insulting you here. I'm only asking you calmly if we can act on the children together."

"You haven't done it yet because you haven't had the chance, but it won't be long. You don't change, you will never change. You're an idiot, yes, an idiot. That's the way it is and there are no other words for it."

"You're the one who's abusing me now!"

"I'm only telling it like it is, which is that you're uncivilized and incapable of improving. It's out of the question for me to accept your decision. I totally disapprove. Furthermore, I also disapprove of how the children are being brought up, the people who are taking care of them, and the way they dress."

"Whatever you think of me, this has to do with our children. What do you suggest?"

"I'm not suggesting anything to you. Nothing will change because you don't change. I think it's important to talk to people but not to you, because you're unreasonable. You don't even know what you're saying. You'll say anything."

"But we have to come to a decision about our children."

"Well, since we're supposed to talk to our equals, why don't you talk to God? I don't happen to have his number—I'm not in the habit of calling. I have nothing more to say. I'll think about it and maybe give you an answer. Anyway, it's useless, because it won't be what you want and you only do what you want. It just won't fly."

"You're making everything impossible before anything happens."
"Yes, because nothing will work with you. I don't want to discuss it with you. You, and what you have to say, don't interest me. Good-bye, madam!"

Seeing the turn the conversation was taking, Elaine taped it. She couldn't believe her ears and went into therapy soon after. She wasn't sure if she was crazy to feel such violence directed toward her or if Pierre still really wanted to annihilate her after five years of separation.

Elaine was right to tape the conversation because it gave her some perspective. Like most victims of stalking, she can't believe that anyone would hate her so much for no good reason. As we can see from their conversation, anything goes with Pierre—sarcasm, abusive language, whatever it takes—when it comes to blocking communication between them. He tries to show that Elaine is a nonentity and responsible a priori for the failure of any course of action. He obstructs change, even that which affects his children, because change would undoubtedly destabilize him. What we also see is envy. Pierre envies Elaine in an infantile manner. She symbolizes the all-powerful mother (the children do just what she wants). She's all-powerful in her closeness to the gods; when he uses that figure of speech, it is said in a frenzy.

I advised Elaine to be careful, after hearing his brutal words spoken in a tone of such icy fury, because I realized Pierre's hatred would never stop. Once unleashed, such hatred becomes an autonomous force. Reason and argument will change nothing. Because a respectable façade is important to the abusive narcissist, only the law can limit the scope of his violence. To be sure, the tape has no legal validity in court, since it's against the law to record private conversations without consent. It's a shame, because emotionally abusive violence really does come through on the telephone. Without physical presence or looks, the aggressor can use his favorite weapon: words, which wound without leaving clues.

The ultimate weapon for the abusive individual is the refusal to communicate directly. Going forward unprotected, the partner is obliged to make demands and give answers, and obviously makes mistakes that are picked up by the aggressor to underline the victim's worthlessness.

The use of powerful allusions and innuendoes in letters is an effective way of unsettling and destabilizing without leaving traces. An outside reader (like a psychologist or judge) can only suppose from this piece of evidence that it's simply an acrimonious but normal exchange between a once-married couple. In this case, no exchange exists. It is unilateral aggression in which the victim is prevented from reacting and defending herself.

This abusive hostility destabilizes families. Children and other witnesses cannot imagine that such violence would be groundless. The victim simply must be partially responsible. In Elaine's case, despite her excellent relationship with the children, every letter causes tension and hostility. "We're fed up with having you in a bad mood every time you get a letter from Dad!" they say. They are also on edge in sensitive situations that might elicit a letter, like a long-distance booby trap. The aggressor can disclaim any hand in the matter and say he's squeaky clean. It's his crazy ex-wife's fault: she doesn't know how to discipline or raise the children.

This is Elaine and Pierre's situation as of now. No end is in sight because a genuinely perverse abuser never lets go of his victim. He is convinced he's right and feels neither scruples nor remorse. His targets must remain permanently irreproachable with no visible faults; otherwise, a new perverse attack may arise.

It took Elaine a long time to understand that what had occurred wasn't a series of misunderstandings in a heated separation; the situation was caused by Pierre's pathological behavior which, in turn, brought about her pathological behavior. With no possibility of a dialogue, they and the children are swept up in a destructive vortex. Stopping the process requires outside intervention.

Elaine kept asking herself, "How am I responsible, either because of my behavior or because of who I am, for this attitude?" She understands now that Pierre is only reenacting what he experienced during his childhood and saw taking place in his family; she, too, has experienced difficulties in shedding the role of healer and mender assigned to her as a child. She was attracted to the "unhappy little boy in need of help" side of Pierre. She is now trapped by what initially seduced her.

EMOTIONAL ABUSE IN FAMILIES

Emotional abuse in families creates an impenetrable correlation of circumstances that is passed on between generations. We are now in the realm of a devastating psychological form of abuse that frequently goes unnoticed by those around it.

Sometimes this abuse is hidden behind the "education mask." Alice Miller denounces the harm caused by traditional education, which aims to break a child's will in order to mold a docile and obedient human being.[2] Children cannot react when faced with "the crushing force and authority of adults, which makes them unable to speak and can even cause them to lose consciousness."[3]

The International Convention of the Rights of Children considers the following as harmful psychological treatment of children:

- Verbal violence
- Sadistic and corrupting behavior
- Rejection of love and affection
- Excessive or disproportionate demands, relative to the child's age
- Contradictory or impossible educational instructions

This violence, never harmless, can be either indirect, or directly aimed at the child an abuser wants to annihilate.

INDIRECT VIOLENCE

In indirect violence, the aggressor generally targets the spouse she seeks to destroy, and violence eventually carries over to the children. Children are victims because they are there and refuse to break their ties to the targeted parent. They are attacked as children of "the other." Called on as witnesses in this conflict that has nothing to do with them, they receive all the evil intended for the other parent. The injured partner, in return, unable to express himself vis-à-vis the abuser, takes out all this pent-up aggression on the children. The children, faced with the permanent disparagement of one parent by the other, have no choice but to isolate themselves. They will lose the possibility of individualization or independent thinking. If they can't find answers on their own, each one of them will carry within a part of suffering that will reappear later.

Hate and destruction are moved elsewhere. The attacker, unable to restrain his unwholesome morbidity, transfers the hatred from the loathed partner onto the children who, in turn, become the target to be destroyed.

Until their divorce, Nadia's parents habitually set their children against each other using a kind of under-the-surface violence. Dirty linen was aired in this family, but always insidiously. The mother knows better than anyone how to use malicious words and insinuations. Her indirect attacks leave poisonous traces in her children's memories.

Since the departure of her husband, Nadia's mother lives alone with her daughter Lea, and suspects the other children of being their father's accomplices. She senses a gigantic plot weaving around her, with Lea at its center, although still a part of her. When Nadia sends Lea a birthday present, her mother answers with "Your sister and I thank you." She communicates her resentments and suspicions to Lea and isolates her from the rest of the family, co-opting her to the point that Lea is indignant when her brothers and sisters continue to see their father.

When Nadia gives her a scarf for Christmas, she'll say, "Your present is the first one I've received from my children today." When her son-in-law commits suicide, she says, "He was weak, anyway; it's better he should leave."

Nadia feels she's dreaming when she sees or hears her mother. Every aggression is perceived as an intrusion, and she needs to protect herself to safeguard her integrity. Her own violence increases with every attack, and with it, the desire to crush her mother so she will stop being "all-powerful" and blaming everyone. As a result of this, she develops stomach pains and digestive problems. Even at a distance, by mail or telephone, she feels a long, prehensile arm reaching out to harm her.

Because abusive manipulation causes serious disorders in children and adults, this behavior, for whatever reason, is unacceptable and inexcusable. How can a child think soundly when one parent says one thing, and the other says just the opposite? If this mental confusion isn't cleared up by the common sense of another adult, the child or adolescent risks self-destruction. There are too many cases involving adults who, as children, have been the victims of various forms of parental abuse, such as incest, and who later suffer from anorexia, bulimia, and other addictive behaviors.

Abusive remarks and allusions create an environment of negative conditioning or brainwashing. Children who are victims of such abuse don't complain about their mistreatment; on the contrary, they endlessly seek approval, which is unforthcoming, from the rejecting parent. They create a negative self-image (I am a nothing), which they accept as being deserved.

Stephen is aware of the fact that well before his depression, he felt empty and incapable of being a self-starter. Although he doesn't even like drugs, he takes them regularly to hide his emptiness and boredom.

Until puberty, Stephen was talkative, lively, happy, and a good student. When he was ten, his parents divorced and he lost his spontaneity. He didn't feel welcome by either parent. His brother decided to live with their mother, so Stephen felt obliged to go with their father. He was a hostage of the divorce.

His father is a cold, discontented, unaffectionate man, full of sarcasm, irony, and hurtful words. He doesn't enjoy life and doesn't want anyone around him to enjoy it, either. Stephen never tells him about his projects. He is a shadow of himself around his father, and when his father leaves him, he thinks, "I can relax now, everything went okay."

Even now, as an adult, Stephen is scared of his father. "If I were the only one to react like this around him, I'd think I was crazy, but no one who comes in contact with him discusses anything because they're afraid of an argument." He's always on his guard, because if his father goes too far in telling him off, he's liable to lose it.

He knows that in general he submits too easily to authority because he can't stand conflict; he also recognizes that even at his age, if he didn't give in to his father, their relationship would break off. He doesn't feel up to confronting him yet.

A parent has a pliable living thing to humiliate right at hand, just as he or she was, or continues to be, humiliated. The child's joy is unbearable. He has to be bullied no matter what; there is a need to make him pay for what the parent has suffered.

Daniel's mother can't stand to see her children happy, since she herself has an unhappy marriage. She's always saying, "Life is a pile of shit. You have to eat crow every day." Having children means sacrificing yourself willy-nilly, and not being able to live a full life.

She is permanently ill-humored and shoots wounding darts at everyone in her vicinity. She's invented a family mealtime game to toughen up her children, which consists of systematically making fun of one of them. The one in the hot seat has to be a good sport. The wounds are tiny, not serious enough to be talked about, but hurtful because they are repeated. The children aren't even sure they're deliberate; maybe Mom is just tactless.

She does nothing but bad-mouth one or the other, indirectly and in disguise, and she fosters rivalry and misunderstandings between them by tearing one down in front of the other.

Looking concerned, she'll say that Daniel is a good-for-nothing and that he'll never amount to anything. Whenever he voices an opinion, she cuts him down in no uncertain terms. As an adult, Daniel still continues to hear his mother's words. He doesn't know how to defend himself against her. He says, "One can't be tough with one's own mother!" He suffers from a recurring dream where he grabs his mother by the shoulders and shakes her, asking, "Why are you so mean to me?"

It's very easy to manipulate children. They only find excuses for the people they love. Their tolerance is unlimited; they are ready to forgive their parents everything and take the blame themselves. They want to understand and try to know why one of their parents is miserable. Blackmail through suffering is a method frequently used to manipulate children.

Celine tells her father that she has been raped and is going to court. Thanks to Celine's composure, the rapist was apprehended and there will be a trial. Her father's first reaction is to say, "You'd do well not to mention this to your mother. Poor thing, it's only one more worry."

Victoria never stops complaining about her stomachache. It gives her an excuse to lie down all day and avoid sex with her husband. She offers her son the following explanation: "You were such a huge baby, you tore my guts out!"

The aggressor's conjugal partner, who is also under her control, can seldom hear about their children's suffering without becoming an advocate for his spouse and justifying his own actions: he is not in a position to help. Early on, the children are aware of the abusive parental relationship, but because they are dependent, they can't acknowledge it. The situation worsens when the other parent, desperate to protect himself, withdraws, leaving the child to face contempt and rejection alone.

Agatha's mother habitually makes her children responsible for all her unhappiness, simultaneously erasing any trace of blame on her part. She says things so calmly that her attacks seem to be the fruit of their imagination. Nothing is acknowledged in this family setup. She says, in effect, "Nothing really happened; you're the one who's letting off steam!"

Only a hazy memory of the violence remains. Little is ever directly said. Agatha's mother dodges and avoids talking. She brings the children over to her side against the husband who deserted her. Unsettled, Agatha doubts her own feelings.

The children know their mother has a box full of their baby pictures under her bed. She says she's thrown them out. Agatha dares to ask her one day what's become of the box. Talking about the box is a way of getting out from under her hold, daring to question the truths forced on them by their mother. She answers, "I don't know, I'll go look—maybe."

Agatha feels like an orphan. Two human beings exist who are her parents but there is no bond between them. She has no comforting shoulder to lean on. She must continually justify herself about everything in order to protect herself from future blows.

DIRECT ABUSE

Direct abuse is a testament to conscious or unconscious parental rejection. The parent justifies himself by explaining that it's all in the child's best interests, as a disciplinary goal. In reality the child disturbs the parent and his spirit must be crushed so that the parent can save himself.

The child only senses this, but the destruction is real. The child is miserable but objectively has nothing to complain about except ordinary gestures and words. People just say the child isn't comfortable with himself. Nevertheless, there is a genuine will to quash the child.

This ill-treated child is considered troublesome. He is a disappointment and a trial to his parents: "That child is difficult; he fails at everything and does stupid things the minute my back is turned!"

A disappointing child is not what this parent had in mind. He is upsetting because he often occupies a special niche in a problematic parental relationship (an unwanted child respon-sible for an unwanted marriage) or he may simply be different (he may have an illness or learning disabilities). Just his pres-ence reactivates parental conflict. He becomes a target to be straightened out and set right.

Bernard Lempert describes very well this rejection that bat-ters an innocent victim: "This lack of love, in certain families, is a systematic destruction that batters a child and makes him want to die; it's not simply an absence of love but an organized violence that the child not only endures but internalizes, to the point where he shifts the violence exerted upon him into self-destructive behavior."[4]

We are caught in an irrational cycle: the parent berates the child for his clumsiness, which just makes him clumsier and further than ever from the parental ideal. The child is not de-valued because he's clumsy, although he becomes clumsy be-cause he's been devalued. The rejecting parent looks for and always finds justifications (bed-wetting, bad grades) for the vio-lence that he feels, but it's the child's very existence and not his behavior that causes it.

One ordinary way of expressing this violence is to tag the child with a ridiculous nickname. Sarah can't forget that fif-teen years ago, when she was a child, her parents called her "garbage can" because she had a big appetite and always fin-ished everything off. When she became overweight, she was no longer her parents' dream child. Instead of helping her control her appetite, they tried to break her spirit even more.

Sometimes a child is blessed with too much of something in relation to his mother or father: he is too gifted, too sensitive, too curious. The parent expunges what's best in the child in order to cover up his own deficiencies. Assertions become pre-dictions: "You're a good-for-nothing." The child ends up insufferable, foolish, or eccentric, so the parent now has good reason to mistreat him. Under the guise of discipline, the parent erodes the very spark of life in the child which is missing in himself. He shatters the child's will and critical spirit, thus making him incapable of judging his parent.

What children most feel, in any case, is that they don't fit their parents' expectations or, quite simply, that they aren't wanted. They are guilty of disappointing them, shaming them, and just not being good enough for them. Apologetic, they want to atone for their parents' narcissism. It's a lost cause.

Arielle completely lacks confidence, even though she knows she's good at her job. Moreover, she attributes her frequent attacks of dizziness and tachycardia to severe distress.

She has always had trouble communicating with her parents, especially her mother, Helene, with whom she has a difficult relationship. Arielle feels her mother doesn't love her, yet she excuses her mother and blames her own position as eldest in the family for putting her in the front line of maternal abuse.

Arielle says she gets mixed messages from her mother. She doesn't understand them or know how to protect herself. Someone once told her that she was the cause of her parents' quarrels; she then felt guilty and even wrote them a letter of vindication.

She feels her mother's negative conditioning on her, like brainwashing, aimed to put her down. In twisted language, every word of her mother's hides a distortion to trap her daughter. Helene slyly uses a third party to initiate conflicts or uses irony to turn situations around. She suggests things as if she were the only one in the know and inevitably makes Arielle take the blame for any wrong. Arielle is always on edge, asking herself if she's doing the right thing so as not to displease her mother.

One day Arielle finds a letter that she had sent her mother on her birthday pinned up in her mother's closet. The date is underlined, and in the margin is scribbled, "A day late!" Arielle can only conclude, "No matter what I do, it's wrong."

Abuse causes terrible damage in families. Without anyone's being aware, it erodes bonds and identity. Abusive individuals so skillfully conceal their violence that they often come across as terrific people. The unhealthy process becomes even more twisted with the involvement of a third person, generally the other parent, who is also controlled unknowingly.

Arthur is a child much wanted by his mother, Chantal, but not by his father, Vincent. The latter lets his wife take care of the baby. He considers that to be a woman's role. When she spends what he thinks is too much time with the baby, Vincent remarks sarcastically, "You're making a wheedler out of the brat!" The tone of voice of those apparently harmless words makes Chantal feel she's been "caught in the act," even though she remarks that it's perfectly normal.

Another time, while changing Arthur, she's singing him a song and kissing him on the belly. From the doorway, Vincent states that lots of mothers act incestuously with their sons when they're still in the cradle. Chantal jokingly replies that his comment is inappropriate, but from then on, when Vincent is around, she is less spontaneous with her son.

Vincent's rules for bringing up the child are very strict: One should generally ignore children's whims; as long as they're properly fed and changed, let them cry. Children must learn not to touch; a good tap on the knuckles will do the trick. Arthur, who's a sweet and easy baby, gets treated roughly fairly often.

Since Arthur is a fat-cheeked baby, his father calls him "fat brat." This enrages Chantal. In spite of all her entreaties, he continues to call him that even when it's to say nice things. "You're the only one it bothers," he tells her. "Look at him. He's smiling." Family members and friends protest, but Vincent still uses the nickname.

Arthur then has some problems with toilet training. He wets himself until nursery school and wets the bed at night much longer. This drives Vincent crazy, who then spanks him. He really lets his irritation show around Chantal, who, fearing his cold rage, takes it out on her son. She's the one who ends up spanking him. Naturally she feels guilty and reproaches Vincent for being too severe. He answers icily, "But you're the one who hit him. You're the violent one!" Chantal goes into her child's room, takes him in her arms, and consoles him— all the while consoling herself.

The parent doesn't actually kill his child, but annihilates him by diminishing his identity until the child becomes nothing. The parent therefore hypocritically maintains a good self-image as the child loses his self-worth. "When tyranny is domestic and despair individual, the stalking achieves its goal: the sensation of no longer being, the annihilation of the soul. We invariably find a common factor in these cases: no traces, no blood, no body. The dead soul lives on and everything is normal."[5]

Even when parental violence is more obvious, one can't denounce it in court for lack of proof.

Although presumably wanted by both parents, it's apparent from the start that Juliette should not have lived. She is responsible from birth for everything that goes wrong. If she's not good, it's her fault; if the housekeeping is difficult, it's her fault. No matter what she does, she's scolded. When she cries, she's reprimanded and slapped:

"Now you'll know why you're crying!" If she doesn't react, she's told, "We have the feeling you could care less what we say to you!"

Her father so desperately wants her out of the way that once, at the age of nine, she was "forgotten" in the forest after a picnic. Some people picked her up and alerted the police. Her father explained it away by saying, "What do you expect? This child is impossible and spends her time running away." Because Juliette is properly clothed and fed and not openly battered, social services does not take on the case, although it's clear she should be removed from her parents. The mother, submissive to an all-powerful husband, tries to make amends and protect her daughter. She resists as much as she can, threatening to leave with the child, but since she has no outside resources she is forced to stay married to an impossible man.

Despite being subjected to violence, Juliette loves her father. When she's asked how things are at home, she sometimes answers, "Mom is always carrying on, saying she wants to leave."

The only protective mechanism for child victims of emotional abuse is to cut themselves off from the situation; subsequently, their identity erodes, the deep core of their soul dies. Everything left over from childhood is perpetually reenacted as an adult.

Even if all abused children don't become abusive parents, a destructive cycle has been created. Each one of us can act out our inner violence on someone else. Alice Miller[6] shows us how over time, children or victims of control forget the violence they suffered—the will to know must be erased—but the syndrome either reoccurs in them or is taken out on others.

Parents don't just transmit positive values, like honesty and respect for others, to their children; they can also teach them to be suspicious and to play fast and loose with the law on the pretext of resourcefulness. It's the law of the shrewdest. In families where abuse is the rule, there's an ancestral "hero" known for his cunning. If one is ashamed of him, it's not because he broke the law but because he got caught.

LATENT INCEST

Besides the abusive violence that seeks to wear down and ultimately annihilate a child's identity, there are families where an unwholesome atmosphere provokes ambiguous looks, sexual allusions, and unhealthy attachments. In such families, the boundaries between generations are unclear; the banal and the sexual mingle. It is not strictly incest, but what the psychoanalyst P. C. Racamier calls "the incestual."[7] The incestual is a climate: a climate where the breeze of incest blows, without incest actually taking place. It's what I would call *soft* incest. There is nothing legally wrong, but perverse abuse exists without any visible signs:

- It's a mother telling her twelve-year-old daughter about her husband's sexual shortcomings and comparing his sexual attributes to those of her lovers.
- It's a father asking his daughter to regularly serve as an alibi, to accompany him and wait in the car while he sees his mistresses.
- It's a mother asking her fourteen-year-old daughter to examine her genital organs for a rash, saying, "After all, this is just between us girls."
- It's a father seducing his eighteen-year-old daughter's friends and caressing them in her presence.

These attitudes foster an atmosphere of unhealthy complicity. Generational barriers are not respected, and children are not allowed to be children, but are forced to bear witness to adult sexuality. This kind of exhibitionism is often dismissed as

50   being modern and "with it." The victim can't defend herself;
if she protests, they'll tease her, saying, "You're so uptight!" She
is therefore obliged to retract and accept, at the risk of going
crazy, principles she initially felt were immoral. Paradoxically,
that kind of moral looseness can coexist with strict rules, such
as staying a virgin. Setting up the perverse control system prevents the victim from seeing things clearly and putting an end
to them.

CHAPTER TWO

EMOTIONAL ABUSE IN THE WORKPLACE

B ecause partners have picked each other, an emotionally abusive relationship can be the essential foundation of a couple, but this is not necessarily the case in a business relationship. Even if the context of the two relationships is different, however, they function in a similar fashion. One can therefore use the "couple model" to understand certain behavioral patterns in the workplace.

Violence and abuse originate in companies when envy of power and perversity collide. The overpoweringly destructive examples of emotional abuse in couples are less likely to be found but, unfortunately, the small abuses of daily living that do exist in businesses are largely trivialized or ignored.

In companies, universities, and institutions, harassing or abusive procedures are more stereotypical than in the private arena. They are no less destructive, although the victims are less exposed because they often leave (illness or resignation) in order to survive. Abusive methods began to be denounced in

51

the public arena (business, politics, institutions) by victims who banded together to make it known that the way they were treated was unacceptable.

WHAT IS ABUSE?

By emotional abuse in the workplace, we mean any abusive conduct—whether by words, looks, gestures, or in writing—that infringes upon the personality, the dignity, or the physical or psychical integrity of a person; also, behavior that endangers the employment of said person or degrades the climate of the workplace.

Although harassment in the workplace is a phenomenon as old as work itself, only since the beginning of the '90s has it clearly been identified as a process destroying the working environment, diminishing productivity, and encouraging absenteeism because of the psychological damage it causes. The process has been studied primarily in Anglo-Saxon and northern countries. Heinz Leymann,[1] a Swedish researcher who worked with a group of professionals for a decade, has labeled it "psychoterror." Today, in numerous countries, labor unions, insurance companies, and corporate doctors are beginning to address the problem.

Business, as well as the media, has tended to focus on sexual harassment, which is only one aspect of harassment in a larger sense. This psychological war in the workplace consists of two elements:

- Abuse of power: often quickly revealed and not accepted by the employees
- Emotional manipulation: more insidious and more destructive from the beginning

Emotional abuse and harassment start harmlessly enough and spread insidiously. Initially, the people involved are reluctant to take offense, and gloss over quarrels and bullying. Later, the attacks multiply and the victim is regularly besieged; he is made to feel inferior and submitted to hostile and degrading maneuvers over a long period.

Obviously, one does not drop dead on the spot as a result of these aggressions, but one does lose a part of oneself. One gets home every night worn out, humiliated, and damaged. It's difficult to recover.

Conflicts are normal in groups. A wounding remark in a moment of irritation or stress is not significant, especially when followed by an apology. The destructive element is caused by the repetition of overt provocations and humiliations.

When abuse appears, it's like setting a machine in motion that will pulverize everything in its path. The process is terrifying because it's inhuman: soulless and pitiless. Whether from cowardice, selfishness, or just plain fear, fellow workers keep their distance. When this type of one-sided destructive interaction occurs, the situation will only deteriorate without decisive outside intervention. In critical moments we tend to emphasize already existing factors: a rigid company will become even more rigid, a depressed employee more depressed, an aggressor more aggressive, and so on. We become caricatures of what we already are. A crisis situation can definitely push an individual to give it his or her all to find solutions, but emotional abuse anesthetizes the victim and only aggravates his or her characteristics.

A vicious circle is set in motion. It's useless to try and figure out the origin of the conflict. One even forgets the reasons for it. A series of deliberate behaviors on the aggressor's part is designed to unleash anxiety in the victim; this anxiety will subsequently result in a defensive attitude that generates new attacks. Reciprocal phobic reactions come into play after a certain length of time; just the sight of the hated person provokes icy rage in the one, while seeing the abuser induces fear in the other: an aggressive or defensive conditioned reflex. Fear disposes the victim to behave pathologically, thereby setting up a retroactive alibi for further aggression. He often reacts in a confused and vehement manner. Everything he initiates or undertakes is turned against him by his abuser. The aim of the maneuver is to completely disorient him and bring him to a state of utter confusion and a sense of his serious shortcomings. Senior executives either turn a blind eye to what is happening or simply let events take their natural course.

Even in cases of horizontal harassment (i.e., colleague against colleague), management tends not to intervene. A problem is often not acknowledged until the victim reacts openly with tears or hysterics or misses work frequently. The abusive conflict basically degenerates because the company refuses to get involved, taking the position that "You're adult enough to handle your own problems." The victim feels not only vulnerable and undefended, but also abused by those who know what's going on and don't intervene. The senior executives rarely suggest a direct solution, putting the problem off with "We'll see later." A common response is unilateral transfer to another job within the company. If, at a given moment early on in the process, someone takes control and acts appropriately, the abuse stops.

WHO IS TARGETED?

Contrary to what their aggressors have others believe, victims are not, at the outset, particularly weak or mentally unhealthy individuals. Quite the opposite: harassment is often set in motion when a victim refuses to give in to a boss's authoritarian procedures. She is targeted because of her capacity to resist authority, even under pressure.

Abuse becomes possible when it is preceded by a devaluation of the victim by her attacker, which is accepted as a surety by the group. Depreciation vindicates, after the fact, the cruelty exercised against her, and leads the group to believe she deserves this treatment.

Victims are not usually malingerers; on the contrary, they are often workaholics (indicating a sure form of dependence): caring perfectionists who work late and on weekends and who show up even when sick. They have a pathological need to be present. This work dependence is not necessarily a characteristic of the victim, but is a result of the company's control over its employees.

Employee benefits can sometimes take an abusive turn. For example, since pregnant women can't be fired, the harassment process can begin when a totally dedicated employee announces her pregnancy. The employer right away sees red flags: maternity leave, early departures to pick up the child, absences due to the child's illness. In short, he fears the model employee will no longer be at his disposal.

The victim is stigmatized once the process of harassment gets going. They say she's impossible to work with, has a terrible disposition, or even that she's crazy. They attribute to her character the consequences of the conflict, forgetting what she was before or what she is now in another context. Pushed to the limit, she often becomes what the employer wants her to become. An abused person cannot live up to her potential. Inattentive and inefficient, she opens herself up to criticism because of the declining quality of her work. She can then be dismissed because of incompetence and lack of professionalism.

Some paranoid individuals who seem victimized should not

be mistaken for true harassment victims. They are tyrannical, inflexible individuals who are quick to disagree with coworkers, can't accept criticism, and feel easily rejected. Far from being victims, they can eventually turn into abusers; they can be spotted by their rigidity of character and lack of guilt.

WHO ATTACKS WHOM?

Group behavior is not the sum of the individual behaviors of its members; the group is a distinct entity with its own behaviors. Freud talks about the dissolution of individuality in a crowd and the development of double identification: horizontal vis-à-vis the group, and vertical vis-à-vis the boss.

AN INDIVIDUAL'S ABUSE OF A COLLEAGUE

Groups flatten individuality and are intolerant of differences (a woman in a group of men; a man in a group of women; homosexuality; racial, religious, or social distinctions). It isn't easy for a woman to gain respect in a traditional male preserve: dismissive attitudes, dirty jokes, obscene gestures—these all seem a little sophomoric and everyone laughs, including the women, who have no choice.

By passing a competitive exam, Cathy becomes a police inspector. Even with women representing only one seventh of the police force, she hopes to be admitted to the squad in charge of minors. After an initial disagreement with a colleague, he closes the discussion by saying, "You're only a hole on legs." This makes the others laugh and add their two cents' worth. She doesn't take this lightly, but rather, protests and gets angry. In retaliation, her colleagues isolate her and try to devalue her in comparison to the other female inspectors: "They're competent women who don't act conceited." During a police action, nobody clues her in. She asks questions—how, where, when, in what police precinct—but nobody answers. They say, "You're too new and wouldn't know what to do anyway. You stay here and make the coffee."

She can't get an appointment to discuss the problem with her superiors. How can you talk about something nobody wants to hear? She has to either fight the group or give in. Because she gets mad, she's called difficult. That label becomes a stigma she can't get rid of in any of her positions.

Going off duty one evening, she leaves her gun in a locked drawer, as usual. The drawer is open the next day. She is reprimanded. Cathy knows there is only one person who could have opened the drawer. She asks to see the commissioner in order to clear up the situation. He calls a meeting with the suspected colleague and mentions to Cathy the possibility of a disciplinary sanction. But during the meeting, he forgets to bring up the reason for their get-together and vaguely criticizes Cathy's work. The report is later lost.

A few months later, when her partner and friend commits suicide, nobody comforts her. When she takes a few days' sick leave, she's teased for being weak. Her colleagues remind her that "We're in a world of guys!"

Many companies are incapable of safeguarding an individual's rights, and allow racism and sexism to develop.

In some cases, envy of someone who possesses a quality the others lack (beauty, youth, wealth, charm) sparks the abuse. This would apply to an overqualified young executive whose boss hasn't reached the same educational level.

A tall, beautiful, forty-five-year-old woman, Cecile is married to an architect and has three children. Because her husband has job problems, she finds work to defray their living expenses. Her background has taught her good manners, and how to dress and speak well. Without a diploma, she only lands a boring, unchallenging job. From the start she's segregated from her colleagues, who make all sorts of disagreeable little remarks, like "How can you afford clothes like that on your salary?"

The process is accelerated by the arrival of a new boss, an envious, gruff woman. Cecile becomes the office flunky with anything at all interesting to do taken from her. When she tries to protest, she's dismissed with sarcastic remarks: "Madam makes unreasonable demands and doesn't want to lower herself with menial tasks!" Cecile, never very confident, isn't quite sure what's going on. She initially tries to show her good faith by accepting the most thankless tasks. Then she blames herself. "It must be my fault," she thinks; "I must have acted stupid." The few times she gets angry, her boss tells her coldly that she's difficult.

So Cecile says nothing and becomes depressed. Her husband doesn't really care about her problems since her salary is minimal. Her doctor, a general practitioner to whom she describes her discouragement, fatigue, and lack of interest, sweeps the problem under the rug with Prozac. He is later astonished at its ineffectiveness and sends her to a psychiatrist.

Abuse between colleagues can also stem from a personal history of competitiveness, with one employee trying to assert himself at the expense of another.

For several years, Denise has had a bad relationship at work with her ex-husband's mistress. This uncomfortable situation makes her depressed. She asks, without success, for a transfer. Three years later, due to an office shake-up, she finds herself taking orders directly from this woman who humiliates her on a daily basis, disparages her work, and makes fun of her mistakes. She questions Denise's ability to write and work on the computer. Denise doesn't dare defend herself, and reacts by turning in on herself and making even more errors. Her job is in jeopardy and she tries again to get a transfer from her boss's superior. She is told it will be taken care of, but nothing changes.

Depressed and desperate, she is put on sick leave. While she is away from the job, her condition improves but she has a relapse when a return to work looms on the horizon. For two years she alternates between sick leave and relapses. The doctor in charge does everything he can to clear things up, but management turns a deaf ear to the situation. She is considered psychologically disturbed because of her complaints and frequent sick leaves. There doesn't seem to be a solution for her. Absence from work could continue until retirement, but after an evaluation, the consulting doctor from Social Security pronounces her healthy enough to go back to the job.

In order not to have to return to the office where she's so miserable, Denise considers resigning. But what is she to do at forty-five, when she is basically unskilled? She now talks about suicide.

Conflict between colleagues in these situations is difficult to manage under most circumstances, and businesses are still noticeably inept at dealing with them. Sometimes the process is reinforced by the support of a superior, but gossips attribute the situation to favoritism or sexual favors.

A large number of executives are not skillful managers and their incompetence makes matters worse. Often responsibility is delegated to the person with the most professional background and not the one with the most managerial expertise. Even when competent in other areas, some executives can't motivate a group and seem unaware of problems between co-workers. If they are aware of a situation, they hesitate to act because they haven't the skills to properly intervene. Incompetence becomes a major factor in emotional abuse cases. In the case of harassment between colleagues, the first appeal should be made to one's superior. But in a hostile atmosphere, asking for help is almost impossible. Indifference and cowardice, as well as incompetence, make people hide behind others.

A SUPERIOR ABUSED BY SUBORDINATES

This kind of situation is much rarer. It can happen in the case of an outsider whose style and methods are disapproved of by the group and who doesn't try to adapt or impose himself. Another example might be when an old colleague is promoted without input from his department. In either case, management hasn't sufficiently taken into account the opinions of the candidate's future coworkers.

The situation gets more complicated when the department's objectives haven't been clearly delineated and the tasks of the promoted employee encroach on those of a subordinate.

Muriel was previously executive assistant to the chief director of a large corporation. By dint of intense work and night classes for several years, she is promoted to a highly responsible job within the group.

She immediately finds herself facing the hostility of secretaries with whom she had previously worked. They don't give her mail or messages, lose files, and eavesdrop on private conversations. Muriel appeals to her bosses, who reply that if she can't make herself respected by the secretaries, she doesn't have the ability to become part of management. They suggest a transfer to a job with less responsibility.

A SUBORDINATE ABUSED BY A SUPERIOR

A common situation is when employees are conditioned to accept anything in order to keep their jobs. The company allows an individual to manage his subordinates in a tyrannical or abusive fashion because it suits management or doesn't seem important. The consequences for the subordinate can be severe.

It might simply be an abuse of power: a superior takes advantage of his position in an unrestrained fashion and, afraid of losing control, abuses his subordinates. This is the power of petty tyrants.

It might also be an abusive process from an individual who needs to crush others in order to heighten his own value, or who needs to destroy another individual targeted as a scapegoat. We shall see how, by means of this perverse abuse, an employee can become trapped.

HOW THE VICTIM BECOMES DISARMED

Fear of unemployment alone doesn't explain the submissiveness of emotional abuse victims. Harassing bosses and petty tyrants seeking total control, consciously or unconsciously, use tactics to psychologically strangle their victims and prevent them from reacting. These same methods of entrapment have been used in concentration camps and continue to be an essential element of totalitarian regimes.

To maintain power and control of the other, the harasser uses seemingly harmless stratagems that grow increasingly violent if the employee resists. He first takes away the employee's critical judgment until he no longer knows who's right and who's wrong. He is stressed, abused, and watched over to the point where he's always on alert; most especially, he is not told anything that might make him understand what's happening. The employee is cornered. He continually withstands more abuse until he comes to realize that the situation is intolerable. The methods are always the same, whatever the point of departure and whomever the aggressor might be. The problem is never articulated, and instead of attempting to find a solution, the abuser slyly tries to erode the person's identity. The process is magnified by the group, acting as either witnesses or active participants.

Emotional abuse in the workplace goes through different stages, all of which have the refusal to communicate as a common theme.

REFUSAL TO COMMUNICATE DIRECTLY

The conflict, although subterranean, is played out daily by means of behavior that invalidate the victim. The abuser refuses to explain this behavior. This unwillingness to explain paralyzes the victim who, unable to defend herself, cannot deal with the aggression. By refusing to label and therefore discuss the conflict, the abuser obstructs finding a solution. The process of emotional abuse must prevent the other person from thinking, understanding, and reacting.

Withdrawal from discussion is an effective means of aggravating the conflict while simultaneously gaining influence. It's a way of saying, without words, that one is not interested in the other person, and even that they don't exist. Because nothing is said, anything may be an accusation.

The situation deteriorates further if the victim has a tendency to self-blame. "What did I do? Why is he mad at me?"

Reproaches, when they exist, are vague and fuzzy, leaving room for all sorts of misinterpretations and misunderstandings. Sometimes, to avoid a real reply, they can be contradictory: "I think you're great, dear, but basically you're worthless."

Any attempts to explain only result in vague reproofs.

Covert abuse could lead to communication, but it works beneath the surface in a non-verbal framework: exasperated sighs and shrugs, contemptuous looks, things left unsaid, innuendoes, and malicious or unsettling allusions. This makes it possible to progressively cast doubt on an employee's professional competence, questioning everything he says and does.

Defending oneself is difficult when abuse is indirect. How can one describe looks full of hate? How can one portray innuendoes and implications? Sometimes the victim doubts her own perceptions and isn't sure she's not exaggerating her feelings. She doubts herself. When these strategies are coupled with a lack of confidence in the employee, the employee will lose all self-confidence and withdraw all self-defense.

Not saying hello, talking about the person like an object (one doesn't, after all, talk to things), saying to someone in front of the victim, "Did you get a look? You really have to be out of it to wear clothes like that!" are all part of invalidation. So are ignoring the victim's presence, not addressing her directly, taking advantage of her being out of the office for five minutes to place a Post-it on her desk explaining a job instead of asking directly for the job to be done.

Invalidation also includes indirect criticism under the guise of jokes, bantering, and sarcasm. One can later say, "It's only a joke, and no one ever died of a joke." The language is specious. Every word hides an insult that ricochets back on to the victim.

DISCREDITATION

In order to ruin someone's reputation, all one has to do is insinuate doubt in others ("Don't you think that . . ."). One can afterwards, in some hypocritical speech made up of innuendoes and implications, insert a real misinterpretation that can be exploited to one's advantage.

To further get the better of the other, the target is ridiculed, humiliated, and covered with sarcasm until he loses self-confidence. He is given a grotesque nickname, or ridiculed because of some shortcoming—physical or otherwise. Slander, lies, and malicious innuendoes are used against him. The stage is set for the victim to know what is happening without being able to defend himself.

These ploys come from envious associates who, in order to get themselves out of an awkward situation, find it easier to place the blame on someone else, or managers who think they can motivate their subordinates by humiliating and continually criticizing them.

The abuser is vindicated when the victim gets depressed or cracks: "I'm not surprised; that person was crazy."

ISOLATION

Once the decision has been made to psychologically destroy an employee, in order to forestall any possible defense, the person must be isolated by breaking up potential alliances. It's much more difficult to rebel if you're alone, especially if you've been made to believe that everyone is against you.

Discord is sown through insinuation and preferential treatment, provoking jealousy, and turning people against one another. The destabilizing process is finished off by envious colleagues, and the real aggressor can disavow any responsibility.

Ostracism by colleagues means eating alone in the cafeteria, not being invited with the others for a drink after work, and so on.

When the aggression comes from the hierarchy, the designated victim is gradually deprived of information. He is isolated, not included in meetings, and only knows what's going on in the company from memos. He's virtually quarantined as the process develops. Although his colleagues may be loaded down with work, he's not given any, but that doesn't necessarily mean he can read the paper or leave the office early.

A case comes to mind of a manager in a large governmental agency who was wanted out of the way. He was suddenly assigned without notice to a beautiful office at some distance, but not given any working goals or personal contacts. After a certain length of time under this treatment, he committed suicide.

Isolation rapidly generates much more stress and damage than work overload. Management finds this an easy way to have someone they no longer need resign.

BULLYING

Bullying consists in giving the victim useless or degrading tasks. That's why Sonia, who has an M.B.A., found herself licking stamps in a tiny, airless office.

It also means setting impossible goals, obliging the employee to work late and on weekends writing an urgent report, and then tossing it aside unread.

Bullying can also mean indirect physical aggression, the kind of negligence that causes accidents: heavy objects that just happen to fall near the victim's feet.

PUSHING THE VICTIM INTO MISTAKES

A very effective way to invalidate someone consists in pushing them to make mistakes, not only in order to subsequently criticize or dress them down, but to create a bad self-image as well. An attitude of disdain or provocation can easily lead an impulsive person to anger or aggressive behavior that everyone no-tices. After that, one can say, "You see, that person is com-pletely nuts and disrupts the office."

SEXUAL HARASSMENT

Sexual harassment is another facet of emotional abuse. It can relate to either sex but generally involves women abused by men, usually a senior executive.

The question is not one of obtaining sexual "favors" but of considering the woman as his sexual "object." The aggressor views the sexually harassed woman as being "at his disposal." She should accept this attitude and feel flattered to have been chosen. The harasser can't imagine the coveted woman refus-ing. If she does, she becomes subject to humiliations and at-tacks. It's not unusual for the abuser to say either that *she* se-duced *him*, or that she was willing.

Different types of harassers have been described, but what they all share is the idea of the dominant male, and negative at-titudes toward women and feminism. Categories of sexual ha-rassment that have been identified include:

- General harassment, which consists of treating a woman differently because she is a woman, with sexist remarks and behavior
- Seductive behavior
- Sexual blackmail
- Unwanted sexual attentions
- Imposition of sexual behavior
- Sexual assault[2]

The American system of justice considers sexual harass-ment as sexual discrimination, whereas in France, a violation of the law occurs only when explicit blackmail relating to the job is involved.

A survey done in the United States[3] reports that 25 to 30 percent of students claim to have been the victim of at least one incident of sexual abuse from professors at college (sexist comments, suggestive looks, sexually inappropriate comments or contact).

HOW ABUSE BEGINS

Although pathologically perverse abusers are rare in business life, they can be formidable in their powers of attraction and their ability to draw the other beyond his limits. A power struggle is legitimate between rivals if the contest is fair game. Certain struggles, however, are unequal at the outset. This occurs when a senior executive is involved or when an individual renders his victim powerless to reply to any attack.

ABUSE OF POWER

The abuse is obvious. A senior executive crushes subordinates with his power. It's also often a way for a petty tyrant to increase his self-esteem. To compensate for a fragile self-image, he needs to dominate; his ability to do so is made greater when the subordinate is afraid of losing his job and has no choice but to submit. Company progress justifies everything: impossible-to-negotiate work schedules, urgent overwork, or unclear demands.

Putting systematic pressure on employees is an inefficient and unprofitable management style, since too much stress can lead to professional mistakes and sick leave. A happy workforce is more productive, although often the petty tyrant and even management are under the illusion that pressure produces profits.

In theory, abuse of power is not specifically directed at an individual; it's simply a matter of destroying someone weaker.

68   In certain companies, the trickle-down effect can go from top
management to the petty tyrant.

Abuse of power has always existed but today it is often dis-
guised. Executives talk about autonomy and initiative but still
demand submissiveness and obedience. Employees march to
their company's drummer because they are haunted by management's bottom line, the threat of unemployment, and the
constant reminder of their responsibility and therefore possible blame.

Eve has been working for a year in a family business as a salesperson.
The pace at work is frantic and overtime is not compensated. Even
when there are weekend trade shows, employees are expected to
show up at 8:00 A.M. Monday morning.

The boss is a tyrant and is never satisfied. Everyone must be at his
beck and call. He shouts when things aren't perfect. "If you're unhappy, go and find yourself another job!" There is no way to defend
oneself. These verbal attacks paralyze Eve. She is constantly nau-
seous, and has to take medication and tranquilizers. Exhausted, she
spends her weekends sleeping, trying to recover, but her sleep is
restless and agitated and doesn't help much.

After a particularly overloaded period of work, she has more and
more panic attacks, cries at the drop of a hat, and can't eat or sleep.
Her doctor puts her on sick leave for depression. After a two-month
absence, she is finally ready to go back to work. Upon her return, her
colleagues are icy, and make her question the reality of her illness.
Her desk and computer are gone. The same atmosphere of terror
reigns: unfair reproaches, foul language, humiliating jobs in relation
to her level of competence, and regular criticism of her work.

She doesn't say anything, and cries in the bathroom. At night
she's drained, and at work in the morning she feels guilty, even when
she hasn't done anything, because everyone in the company is on
edge and spying on one another.

Eve describes her job as a stress factory. All her coworkers complain of psychosomatic symptoms—headaches, backaches, colitis, rashes—but like frightened children, they don't dare complain to the boss, who wouldn't pay attention anyway.

Six months after her first sick leave, she is summoned to a preliminary meeting to discuss her getting laid off. The memo arrives following a day off she has taken after feeling sick at a trade show, and triggers something inside her. For the first time, she is angry. She feels the injustice and dishonesty of the situation, and decides she will not be taken advantage of. Despite feelings of guilt and asking herself, "I wonder to what extent I provoked this," she acts.

She gets advice and attends the meeting with an outside lawyer. The official reason given is the loss of confidence in her, as a result of frequent absences without explanation. The lawyer points out that her latest absence was after a trade show when the boss was unreachable. None of the boss's claims provide sufficient reason to fire her. He says he'll think about it because there's all the time in the world to send the letter.

One has to be sure of one's rights in order to defend oneself efficiently. Eve informed herself and also knew what not to do. If she hadn't attended the meeting with a lawyer, her boss would have terrified her as he always had, before condescendingly giving her "another chance."

Eve waits for the letter that will officially fire her. She goes about her work with a certain pleasure, but it doesn't take long for the stressful environment to get the old cycle going. Her situation is even more uncomfortable since the meeting. She receives faxes every day that point out small errors. Her colleagues tell her, "You shouldn't have done that; you've stirred up his anger." She has to justify everything but wisely photocopies important exchanges. She must make sure not to make mistakes or be wrong. She takes her personal papers with her during lunch hour, even if her coworkers make fun of her paranoia. "You're going off to lunch with your book-bag just like a school girl." Some of them throw files on her desk without saying a word. If she protests, they ask, "Do you have a problem?" She shrinks into herself to avoid the teasing. The boss avoids her and gives her instructions in writing.

He begins the laying-off process again a month later, saying that Eve's attitude hasn't changed. Because this time it's established that his only reason for firing her is personal, the personnel lawyer negotiates a financial settlement for her. Afraid that she'll go to arbitration, the boss signs it.

After her departure, Eve learns that five of her colleagues, including three senior staff members, are also leaving. One left for a better offer but the other four simply resigned without benefits.

ABUSIVE SCHEMES AND MANEUVERS

When an abusive individual comes into a group, he gathers around him and seduces the more submissive members. If a particular individual resists getting roped in, he is rejected by the group and designated a scapegoat. Criticism and gossip about the isolated individual bond the group members. They are now vulnerable to influence, and follow the lead of the abusive person in terms of cynicism and disrespect. Individually, they retain their moral values, but because they depend on an unscrupulous leader, they lose all critical sense.

Social psychologist Stanley Milgram studied the phenomenon of submission to authority[4] between 1960 and 1963. His method was the following: A person is asked to perform a series of actions in a psychology laboratory that will increasingly conflict with his conscience. The question is to know precisely up to what point he will follow the experimenter's instructions before refusing to carry out specific actions. In conclusion, Milgram believes that "many ordinary people, without hostility, can become agents of a cruel destructive process simply by doing their job." This finding is taken up by Christophe Dejours,[5] who talks about the social banality of evil. There exist, in effect, some people who require a higher authority in order to reach their equilibrium. Abusive individuals benefit from this submissiveness and use it to inflict suffering on others.

The goal of the abusive individual is to gain or maintain power by whatever means possible or else to mask his own incompetence. In order to accomplish this, he must get rid of anyone who impedes his progress or sees through him. Simply attacking someone weaker won't suffice, as we can see in examples dealing with abuses of power. One must also weaken the other person to prevent him from defending himself.

Fear generates obedience, even submissiveness, in the targeted person, and also affects colleagues, who let the behavior occur and refuse to see what's going on around them. It's the reign of crass individualism: "Every man for himself." The entourage is afraid to show solidarity and become part of the next batch of firings. One mustn't make waves in a company. One must show team spirit and conform.

George Huang's movie *Swimming with Sharks* summarizes all the humiliation and mental agony an eccentric and sadistic boss can inflict on an ambitious employee who is determined to succeed at any price. We see the boss insult his employees, lie unscrupulously, give confusing orders, keep a worker on call day and night, and change the rules in order to keep an employee permanently on edge. Coworkers are forewarned: "Hitting below the belt is not only recommended, but rewarded!" The boss accomplishes this while simultaneously continuing to entice the new recruit with visions of a promotion. "Do this for me. Keep quiet, listen, and take note. You're brainless. Your personal opinions don't count and what you happen to think is totally uninteresting. What you feel is boring. You are here exclusively for me: to protect my interests and respond to my needs. I don't want to make a martyr out of you. I want you to help because if you do your job well, if you listen and learn, then you have the potential to get everything you want."

An emotional abuser works more effectively in an unorganized, poorly structured company. He only needs to find the slightest breach to then widen his search for gratification of power.

The technique never varies: one uses the other's weaknesses to lead him to self-doubt and then to annihilate his defenses. By an insidious process of erosion and abuse, the victim gradually loses all confidence and sometimes becomes so confused that he ends up putting his attacker in the right: "I'm a zero; I can't deal; I'm not up to it!" In this way, the destructive erosion happens unobtrusively until the point where the victim accuses himself.

Miriam is the creative designer at a thriving advertising boutique. In theory, she is solely responsible for her designs, but everything is actually coordinated by a managing director with direct access to the chief executive. Miriam invests a lot of energy and hard work in the job (including unpaid late nights and weekends) because of her design responsibilities. But as soon as she openly exercises too much autonomy by worrying about the final result of her projects, she is put back in her place. The director, who is not a designer, takes a project she has submitted and changes it according to his taste, without warning or consulting her. If she asks for an explanation, he casually answers, with a big grin, "Come on now, Miriam, it's not all that important!" Miriam feels an inner rage she can rarely express: "I worked on that project for three days, and in a few seconds he takes what I've done and makes it unrecognizable without bothering to explain. You'd think I wanted to create for someone who disowns my work!"

There is no way to discuss any of this. Everything is left unsaid. None of the employees can say what they think to this manager; they're all afraid of his temper. The only solution is to constantly dodge the situation. Mistrust creeps in. The employees ask themselves, "What's he getting at?" By using humor and ridicule, he manages to make everyone conform to his expectations. As soon as he arrives on the scene, everyone immediately tenses up and waits to be "caught in the act." Most of the staff, in order to avoid unpleasantness, just end up criticizing themselves.

In view of the increasing workload, the manager has agreed to let Miriam hire an assistant and right away sets them against each other. When Miriam expresses her thoughts about a project for which she is responsible, the manager doesn't listen and, shrugging his shoulders, turns to her assistant: "You probably have a better idea!"

He continually demands more from Miriam and asks that the work be done more and more quickly. If she refuses to turn in something not up to her standards, he blames her for being a difficult person. She ultimately accepts this criticism.

Her resistance produces stress, which causes stomachaches and panic attacks. She feels barely alive at work.

Miriam's manager wants to control everything and refuses to share power. Envy makes him want to appropriate Miriam's designs. This management style, when it works, creates an all-powerful boss. Some people adapt to this infantilism, and conflicts between colleagues become spats between siblings. Miriam resists but can't make herself follow through entirely because she's afraid of losing her job. She is, however, unmotivated and very affected by the whole situation. "I can really understand why a person commits murder; I feel impotent and dangerously violent!"

While some employers treat their personnel like children, others treat them like things—to be used at will. In a case like Miriam's, where creativity is involved, the attack on the person is even more direct: any initiative or innovation on their part is destroyed. Employers try to prevent the departure of useful or indispensable employees; they mustn't be allowed to think the situation through or feel capable of working somewhere else. They must be led to believe they're only worth their present job. If they resist, they're isolated. They are denied any kind of contact: eye contact, greeting in the hall, or a deaf ear turned to their suggestions. Hurtful and unkind remarks come next, and if these prove insufficient, emotional violence appears.

Outright hostility later replaces latent ill-will or malevolence if the victim reacts and tries to rebel. This is the phase of emotional abuse that has been called "psychoterror." At this stage, any means or methods will be used, sometimes including physical violence, to destroy the designated victim. This can lead to psychical annihilation or suicide. The attacker has now lost sight of any potential benefits to the company and focuses only on his victim's downfall.

During the abuse process, there exists not only the element of a search for power, but also the special pleasure taken in using the other as an object or puppet. The aggressor reduces his victim to a condition of such powerlessness that he then is able to destroy him with impunity. He'll use any device to obtain what he desires, especially if it means hurting other people. To gain self-esteem by humbling others seems totally legitimate. There is no respect for them. What strikes one the most is the limitless hatred an abuser feels for no apparent reason and his complete lack of compassion for people trapped in unbearable situations. The aggressor who inflicts violence on another person believes she deserves it and has no right to complain. The victim is only an annoying object whose identity must be eroded to the point of denying its existence. There is no acknowledgment of feelings or emotions on her part.

The victim must face this aggression alone, which she doesn't understand; in most abusive situations, the circle of people nearest the conflict show cowardice and complacency because they are afraid of being targeted in turn, or sometimes take a kind of sadistic pleasure at the sight of this abuse. In a normal relationship, it's possible to use conflict when necessary and limit the supremacy of one party, thereby imposing a balance of power. However, an emotional abuser cannot bear the slightest opposition to his power and will transform a conflicted relationship into hate, desiring the destruction of the other person.

Lucy has worked for ten years as a sales manager for a small family enterprise. Because she was involved at the outset, she's very attached to the company. Initially it was a real challenge to find clients.

The boss was always a wheedling, paternalistic "monarch," but since the business has prospered, he has become totally tyrannical and despotic. He doesn't say good-morning when he arrives or look his employees in the eye while giving orders; he also insists that office doors remain open, gives instructions five minutes before a meeting, etc. All these factors are emotionally draining because they oblige people to be permanently on alert. To more effectively "rule," he encourages conflict and gossip, flatters those who are more submissive, and opposes those who resist him. Lucy keeps her distance because she feels that what's happening is a real power seizure. Her attitude is considered an act of rebellion.

Everything unravels when the boss hires another sales manager. The boss immediately places the newcomer on a pedestal and treats her with obvious favoritism. Such flagrant injustice, amounting to what seems like attempted bribery, makes the newcomer suspicious and want to resign her job. The boss convinces her not to leave and lets their associates know that the melodrama is caused by Lucy's jealousy.

By putting the two women head to head, the boss figures that they'll attack each other and then he'll be able to control both of them more easily.

Lucy becomes isolated from this point on. She no longer gets information, her work isn't acknowledged, and nothing is ever right. Word spreads that she is incompetent. Although she knows she is a good sales manager, she ends up doubting her capability. She becomes stressed and confused but tries to cover it up because she feels it might be used against her. The other employees keep their distance because if they seem too close to her they will be weakened.

Like many victims of emotional abuse, Lucy is late to react. She had unconsciously assigned the role of father to her boss.

The day she hears him make insulting comments about her to a colleague, she demands a meeting:

"You insulted me; what do you have against me?"

"I'm not afraid of anything or anyone. Leave."

"I won't leave until you tell me what you have against me."

The boss then loses his cool. He turns his desk over in a rage and breaks everything within reach, saying, "You are a total incompetent and I'm sick of your spitefulness!"

Not realizing that she won't give in, the boss plays the "terror card." He reverses their roles and makes himself the victim of an abusive employee.

Lucy, who had for so long felt protected by him, can't understand the contempt and hate she sees in his eyes. But the physical violence triggers a reaction in her and she decides to sue. Her colleagues try to dissuade her, saying, "Stop it. You'll only have problems. He'll calm down in the long run." Shaking and crying, she goes to the police station to lodge a complaint. She then sees a doctor who issues her a note for an eight-day sick leave. At the end of the day, she stops by the office to pick up her briefcase.

Lodging a complaint is the only way to end psychoterror. Because it signals a definitive break with the company, one either has to be at the end of one's rope or has to draw on a lot of courage. Nor is a positive outcome of the process necessarily assured.

THE ORGANIZATION THAT PERMITS ABUSE

This type of example is only possible in a company that encourages or turns a blind eye to abuse. Some managements know what measures to apply in the case of an incompetent, unmotivated employee, but don't know how to deal with a disrespectful employee or one who is unpleasant to an associate. Privacy is respected within the workplace and management follows a "hands off" policy; it considers employees mature enough to work things out amongst themselves, but the consequences show a lack of respect for the individual.

When a company goes along with this attitude, it creates competitive employees who, while not inherently abusive, lose sight of their moral guidelines and allow themselves to be swept up in the process. They are no longer shocked at seeing an individual treated wrongfully or abusively. They no longer recognize the boundary between berating someone to spur them on and harassing them. In a competitive framework, the boundary of respect for a human and the rights of an individual must not be forgotten.

The threat of unemployment allows arrogance and cynicism to creep into management methods. In a fiercely competitive framework, coldness and hardness take over. Competition, by whatever means, is judged healthy and the losers are thrown out. Individuals who fear confrontation don't use direct methods to obtain power. They manipulate the other in an underhanded or cruel fashion in order to obtain his submission. By weakening the victim in this manner, they boost their own self-image.

In this context, an individual greedy for power can use an atmosphere of general confusion to destroy potential rivals with impunity. A single individual unchecked by management can manipulate and erode the identity of other individuals without fear of reprisal in his quest to gain or consolidate power.

Certain characteristics in the workplace will facilitate the introduction of abuse. Unquestionably, conflicts will arise more easily in groups under pressure. Introducing new work methods to increase performance while ignoring the human factor generates stress and creates a favorable atmosphere for abusive conduct.

Initially, stress is a physiological phenomenon in an organism, enabling it to adapt to an attack of whatever nature. In animals, it's a survival instinct. They have the choice, when faced with aggression, to fight or to run. That choice doesn't exist for an employee. His organism, like the animal's, reacts in three successive stages: alertness, then resistance, followed by exhaustion. This physiological phenomenon, however, has lost its original purpose of physical preparedness, giving way to social and psychological adaptation. Employees are asked to work too hard and too fast and to be able to react in many different ways. Medical experts specializing in working conditions analyzed the consequences of flexibility on employees in a slaughterhouse: "It is true," they write, "that economic constraints weigh heavily on the level of activity but, at a closer look, in certain sectors, these economic demands go too far: work becomes ever more speedy, with excessive and atypical schedules and, progressively, an extraordinary lack of consideration enters the picture."

The economic consequences of stress at work and the health

problems that result from it remain insufficiently acknowledged and quantified. Stress is not recognized either as a "professional or working illness" or as a direct reason for absenteeism, although doctors and psychiatrists specializing in the field have established the link between increased psychosomatic ailments, and alcohol and drug abuse, with too much pressure at work.

An unorganized structure always generates stress, whether from: (1) unclear role definition (no one knows who does what or who's responsible), (2) an unstable organizational climate (a person has been assigned a position and no one knows if it's permanent), or (3) a lack of coordination (decisions are made without the agreement of interested parties). The rigidity of certain hierarchical systems allows certain individuals eager for power to move relentlessly against other individuals with impunity.

Some enterprises are "lemon squeezers." They put a false glow on things, they play on people's emotions and always demand more of their workforce. When an employee is worn out and no longer profit-earning, the business gets rid of him without a qualm. The structure of the workplace can be very manipulative. It's not unusual for management to establish relationships that go far beyond normal employee-employer contractual bonds in order to motivate their personnel, although, theoretically, emotions aren't directly played on. Management demands that their employees put heart and soul into the company, using a system that sociologists Nicole Aubert and Vincent de Gaulejac[6] have called "imaginational," thus transforming them into "golden slaves." On the one hand, they are asked to overly give, but also bear the consequences of stress; on the other, there is no recognition of their effort or of them as individuals. They become interchangeable pawns. In some companies, employees never stay very long in a position where they could become overqualified. They are kept in a permanent state of ignorance and inferiority. Any sign of originality or personal initiative is out of place. Motivation and spirit are broken by refusing to give employees any responsibility or further education. The employees are treated like undisciplined students; they can't laugh or relax without being called to order. They are sometimes asked to criticize themselves in weekly meetings, turning working groups into public humiliation sessions.

Aggravating the process is the fact that a number of them are underemployed and have a level of studies equivalent or superior to that of their immediate superior, who then applies pressure until the employee can't take on any more work and ends up blaming himself. Economic constraints mean increasing demands on employees, with less and less consideration for their well-being. The person and his knowledge are devalued. The individual doesn't count. His history, his dignity, and his suffering are of little importance.

Most employees confronted by this phenomenon of "thingness" and of robotic approach feel their hold on the situation is too fragile to do anything but protest inwardly and bow their heads while hoping for better times. It's not unusual for an employee to refuse the sick leave suggested by his doctor to battle stress and the attendant insomnia, fatigue, and irritability: he is afraid of reprisals on his return.

There are several ways of getting rid of an employee without specific grounds:

- Eliminate his job in a company restructure based on economic need.
- Give him a very difficult task and then look for weaknesses in his performance, creating a legitimate reason for letting him go.

· Use emotional abuse to make him break, which will result in voluntary resignation.

Emotional abuse often takes place when an employee is weakened by some external cause. If, for personal reasons (a divorce, for example), he seems less available on the job, he is insidiously blamed for things he'd never been previously blamed for. What had been accepted is no longer accepted because of the feeling that the individual has let his guard down. The instigators of the abuse are then convinced that they're in the right and the person is truly incompetent. Using another person's weakness is a valuable strategy, commonly used in business and politics. Self-congratulation is in order for success in a "world of sharks" and a "dog-eat-dog" environment.

Oliver is a senior partner in a large law firm. The firm has grown tremendously since its inception, and lots of young graduates have recently arrived on the scene, expecting quick success. The other senior partner in the group, Frank, an old friend, has a Byzantine management style. Oliver doesn't participate in his schemes, which he disapproves of, but doesn't want to put their association in jeopardy because it's a mark of success for the firm.

One day he hears a rumor from his associates that someone is out to get him and that he could expect trouble from a group of discontented employees because of a litigation process that Frank has launched. He asks Frank, who answers by attacking: "If you want trouble, go ahead and find it. I know nothing about anything!"

Oliver has always known that this man doesn't respect anyone. He uses other people by luring them with dreams of power and stirs up conflicts among junior partners in order to consolidate his position. The office atmosphere reeks with subterranean fighting and corruption. Young associates, sensing this, prefer to leave because they know that if a clash occurs, the latest arrivals are the most vulnerable.

Frank either blocks files or assigns them to more malleable associates to unsettle Oliver. Oliver defends himself badly at the beginning. Even knowing his old university buddy's rigid management style, Oliver can't believe he would act this way toward him. Oliver finally reacts and plans his defense strategy when he discovers that Frank has drawn money from the firm account without forewarning him.

THE ORGANIZATION THAT ENCOURAGES ABUSIVE METHODS

When the end justifies the means and anything goes, the company itself can become an abusive system, ready to destroy to attain its objectives. In these cases, because of the twisted values prevalent in the workplace, lying enables the abusive process to take root.

In a competitive economic system, executives often can only fulfill their responsibilities by clinging to a destructive management system and refusing to acknowledge the human factor. They deal in lies and fear. An individual's abusive maneuvers can be consciously used by a company that wants to increase profits.

The factory of a small clothing company in France is an example of this management style. The personnel, including the chief executive, are all women. The manager is the sole male. This petty tyrant feels nothing but contempt for the workforce: he humiliates, harms, and injures them in the name of production efficiency. His methods include harassing the employees to work faster and increase output, timing breaks, and insulting everyone, all done in complicity with the female chief executive, who is fully aware of his methods and keeps quiet.

The workers go on strike, but before the conflict comes to a head, television cameras film the factory, focusing on the manager. Even while being filmed, he doesn't change his humiliating tactics: he considers them totally legitimate and right. He doesn't question himself for a second. When a strike explodes, 85 out of 108 employees come out of the factory to demand the manager's resignation. They finally get it, but not before 64 workers are let go. The manager, whose management style was openly condemned by the media, soon found a job in a factory twice as big.

Power can be a terrible weapon when held by an abusive system or individual.

Clemence is a beautiful young woman with a business degree. After graduation, she worked on a short-term contract and then became unemployed. It was therefore a huge relief when she was hired by a successful company as director of marketing and communication, replacing the new chief executive. She is the only female executive. Initially she reports to an associate, who leaves, and then directly to the president.

At this point he begins to bully her: "What you've done is worthless!" "One would think you don't know anything about marketing!" No one has ever spoken to her this way before but she doesn't dare say anything for fear of losing a job that she finds interesting.

He appropriates her suggestions and then implies that because she doesn't show initiative, she's a nothing. When she protests, he gets irritated: "Just keep quiet and work!" He never gives her a job directly; he puts a file on her desk with instructions attached. He never encourages her or congratulates her on a job well done.

Her associates in the company, mostly men, identify with the president and begin to avoid her and speak ill of her. Because the offices are open, everyone spies on one another. It is much more difficult to defend oneself.

One day she dares approach the president. He doesn't answer and looks away as if he hasn't heard. When she persists, he acts like the village idiot: "I don't understand what you're talking about!"

Even though her job is in communication, she's forbidden to bother people by talking to them face to face. E-mail is the only allowable form of communication.

Telephones and computers in this company are locked by codes. Absent on sick leave for a few days, she returns to find the codes changed and has to wait for a secretary, who's very close to the president, to unlock her equipment. She objects: "You could have put everything back in place if you used my office!"

"Don't give me a pain; I don't know who you think you are; everybody knows you're paranoid!"

Later she learns that important telephone calls have been short-circuited, on the president's orders, by this same secretary. An e-mail exchange follows between the secretary and Clemence, with a copy to the president. Deliberately ignoring Clemence, he only reassures the secretary, who had been afraid of bothering him.

Little by little, Clemence loses her self-confidence. She questions her behavior: "What have I done for them to treat me this way?" A brilliant graduate, she begins to doubt her professional ability. She sleeps badly, dreading Monday mornings when she has to go to work. She has migraines and crying jags, which she describes to her husband at night. She loses her spirit, and doesn't want to go out or see her friends.

Companies often turn the other way in relation to abusive behavior if it can generate profits and not cause trouble. But companies should be catalysts for development, not instruments of destruction.

In the movie *Harassment* by Barry Levinson, we see how a company enables the attempted destruction of one individual by another. The story takes place in a Seattle company specializing in electronic chips. After merging with a company in computer programming, the business needs a chief executive officer. Meredith (Demi Moore) unexpectedly gets the promotion at the expense of Tom (Michael Douglas), who was more experienced and qualified for the job. One might expect her to quietly gloat over her victory because she's always been jealous of other people's happiness. On the contrary, it's "off with his head!" Tom is a healthy, happy man with a sweet wife and two great kids. Meredith, formerly his mistress, can't take away this simple happiness, so she elects to annihilate him using sex as a weapon. She makes passes at him, which he rejects. She seeks revenge herself by accusing him of sexual harassment. In cases like this, sexual aggression becomes a means of humiliating another person, treating him like an object, and ultimately destroying him. If sexual humiliation isn't enough, she'll find other ways of "demolishing" her victim.

In this film, we witness not only the struggle for power as waged by an abusive narcissist, but also the need to appropriate or, if that's impossible, to destroy, another's happiness. The tools the abuser uses are the other's faults and weaknesses; if they're not sufficient to achieve the goal, she will create others.

Whether the starting point lies in a conflict between individuals or in the inept structure of an organization, it's up to the company to find a solution; a company policy of noninterference allows the abuse to happen. There is always a moment in the process when the company can intervene with the solution. In spite of the presence today of human resource directors, few companies take into account the human factor and, even less so, the psychological dimensions and implications of relationships in the workplace.

Nevertheless, the economic consequences of abuse are not unimportant for a company. Deterioration of the work climate carries with it dramatically less efficiency of output of a group or team. Handling the conflict becomes the main preoccupation of attackers and victims, and sometimes even the witnesses, who can no longer concentrate on work. The losses for the company become significant, because of both the decrease in the quality of work and the increase of hidden costs due to absenteeism.

Sometimes an inversion of the process occurs. The organization becomes the victim of its managers. It is sucked dry by predators whose only concern lies in maintaining a system that increases and enhances their own value.

Abuse is always the result of conflict. It is important to know if it stems from the characters of the people involved or if it's inherent in the structure of the company. Not all conflict degenerates into abuse; for that to occur, several factors are necessary:

· Dehumanization of relations at work
· All-powerfulness of the company
· Tolerance toward or complicity with the abusive
  individual

In the workplace, it's the decision-makers as a whole (managers, "executive suite," directors of the board) who must choose to intervene, to refuse to accept abuse, and to ensure that human dignity is respected at every level of the company. Even without laws regulating emotional abuse or moral and sexual harassment, they are obligated to impose respect for individuals and to exclude racism and sexism from the company. Labor unions, whose role is to defend workers, should include effective protection against emotional abuse and other kinds of personal attacks on the individual.

Let's not trivialize abuse by making it an inevitability in our society. It is not economically linked, but stems instead from lax attitudes in organizations.

PART II

THE
ABUSIVE
RELATIONSHIP

CHAPTER THREE

EMOTIONALLY ABUSIVE SEDUCTION

From the study of clinical cases, we now know that an emotionally abusive relationship goes through two phases: (1) identity erosion, and (2) open violence.

The first phase, which the psychoanalyst P. C. Racamier has termed "brainwashing,"[1] can take place over several years. It builds progressively through a seduction process at the beginning of a relationship. The victim is destabilized and gradually loses self-confidence during this initial phase.

Stalking is the first step, followed by a period of using influence on the victim in order to finally control him and leave him without a shred of autonomy.

The seductive process consists not only in overpoweringly winning over the person, but also in corrupting and suborning him. The manipulator bypasses reality, operating secretly and by surprise. He attacks underhandedly, gaining the admiration of another person, who is dazzled by him and sends back to him a positive image. The stalking process uses another's protective instincts. Because it is narcissistic seduction, the abuser

89

seeks to find in another person a favorable self-image and a fascination with his persona without allowing himself to be taken in. For J. Baudrillard,[2] this single-minded seduction wards off reality and manipulates appearances. It's not positive energy, but a malevolent process, almost like a ritual. Narcissistic seduction confuses and erodes the boundaries of one's own identity and that of another individual. This is not the world of transference—for example, when a lover's idealization, in order to sustain passion, refuses to acknowledge any shortcomings in the beloved—but a world of incorporation where the objective is to destroy. The other's presence is considered threatening and not complementary.

The period of influence consists in leading someone, without argument, to think, make decisions, and behave other than he would spontaneously on his own. During the "seductive stalking" period, the targeted person is unable to freely consent a priori because his sensibilities and vulnerabilities are influenced and manipulated. As in any manipulative process, the victim must first be made to believe he is free, even when he is insidiously deprived of the freedom to act. There can be no question of a discussion between equals; the abuser must subtly impose himself while preventing the other from becoming aware of the process and from discussing or resisting it. The victim's ability to defend himself is withdrawn, and his judgment is negated, thereby eliminating any possibility of rebellion. We find here the types of situations in which one individual exerts undue and abusive influence over another without his knowledge. In daily life we are constantly being manipulated, destabilized, and muddled, and every time it happens we are furious at the perpetrator but even more ashamed of ourselves.

Control is intellectual or spiritual domination in a power relationship. Power draws the other into a situation of dependency, that is, acquiescence and attachment. Eventually, veiled threats and intimidation become part of the picture. The victim must be weakened and made vulnerable in order to more easily assimilate ideas and suggestions. To force acceptance of something on another person acknowledges a basic inequality. The tentacles of control can reach into another person's soul and brain. As stated in the *DSM-IV*,[3] personality dissociation can be triggered by prolonged situations involving coercive persuasion techniques such as brainwashing, ideological reorientation, or prisoner indoctrination.

Control exists only in the domain of relationship: it is the intellectual or moral domination, influence, or ascendance of one individual over another.[4] The victim is caught in a spiderweb, held captive at another's disposal, bound psychologically, and anesthetized. He is completely unconscious of what's happened.

There are three main elements in seizing control:

- An act of appropriation by dispossessing another person
- An act of domination, whereby the other person is kept in a state of submission and dependence
- An element of branding, whereby one leaves one's mark on another

Control inherently contains an unquestionably destructive dimension because it negates the desire of another person and erodes his or her identity. Little by little, victims see their resistance and potential to oppose eaten away. They lose all critical ability. Prevented from reacting, literally "shattered," they are made accomplices to their oppression. This has nothing whatsoever to do with consent. They are transformed into an object; they can no longer think for themselves but must think like their aggressors. They are not separate and distinct other selves or alter egos, and they submit to their abusers without consent or participation.

Initially, according to seductive stalking strategy, the other person is not directly destroyed with one blow, but is kept at the attacker's disposal and obliged to submit very gradually. What matters is maintaining power and control. The maneuvers seem harmless at first, but become more and more insidiously violent as the partner resists. When the partner is too docile and submissive, the game is not exciting. There must be enough resistance for the aggressor to want to maintain the relationship, but not so much as to threaten him. He must call the game plays. The other is not an interactive subject, but merely a useful object who must stay that way.

All victims describe an inability to concentrate when the persecutor is nearby. The persecutor makes sure of seeming totally innocent to a neutral observer. There is an enormous discrepancy between the victims' apparent comfort and their real discomfort and suffering. They complain, at this stage, of feeling smothered and of not being able to do anything on their own. They describe the sensation of not having room to think.

At first, they obey to please their partner or to make him feel better because he seems unhappy. Later, they obey because they are afraid. Children especially accept submission at the beginning as a need for recognition and because it is preferable to abandonment. Because an abuser gives little and asks a lot, there is implicit blackmail in the relationship or, at the very least, doubt arises in the victim's mind. "If I become more submissive, he will finally appreciate or love me." It's an endless search, because the aggressor cannot be gratified. On the contrary, the victim's quest for love and recognition unleashes the hatred and sadism of the abusive narcissist.

It's a paradoxical situation, because the more the aggressor battles his fear of the other's power (a fear that becomes almost overpowering if he feels the other is superior), the more control he seeks to exact.

During the control phase, the victim will feel relatively at ease if she behaves submissively and allows herself to be caught in a web of dependence. A subterranean current of violence has been established that will easily become overt. The situation between the protagonists is rigid, with no possible change. The fear they feel for each other maintains an uneasy status quo:

- The aggressor is blocked either by an inner loyalty based on his personal history that prevents him from acting straightaway, or by his deep-seated fear of the other.
- The victim is blocked by either the control that has taken place and its resultant fear, or a refusal to acknowledge her rejection by the aggressor.

During this phase, the aggressor maintains a state of tension in the relationship, putting the victim in a state of permanent stress.

The control exerted is not generally apparent to outside observers. They are oblivious to what's happening and blinded even when faced with the evidence. For those who don't understand the abusive context and its innuendoes, the destabilizing allusions don't come across for what they are. After this phase, an isolating process occurs. This victim has been cornered into a defensive posture which makes her behave in a manner that

94 irritates the people around her. She can become shrewish, whiney, or obsessive. In any case, she loses all her spontaneity. Those close to her don't understand what is causing her behavior and are led to judge her negatively. Communication during this isolating process takes on a special slant involving lies, sarcasm, ridicule, contempt, and self-contradictory attitudes.

CHAPTER FOUR

COMMUNICATION IN AN EMOTIONALLY ABUSIVE RELATIONSHIP

E stablishing firm control requires procedures that give the illusion of communicating—a singular kind of communication that doesn't really aim to connect but, on the contrary, aims to maintain a distance that will prevent meaningful exchange between the partners. The goal of this distorted communication is to enable the other person to be used. He must be verbally manipulated in order to keep him in the dark about the process and make him even more confused. A virtual "blackout" on real information is an essential element in reducing the victim to a state of powerlessness.

Violence, even when it is non-verbal, hidden, and smothered, can be transmitted by what is unspoken or implied, and will result in considerable anguish.

REFUSAL OF DIRECT COMMUNICATION

There is never direct communication because "one just simply doesn't discuss things."

Abusive individuals evade a direct question when it is asked. Because they won't talk, one ascribes wisdom and grace to them. One enters a world with little verbal communication and vague unsettling remarks. Everything is suggested but never said outright. A shrug of the shoulders or a sigh will suffice. The victim tries to understand: "What have I done to him? Why is he reproachful?" And because nothing is actually said, anything becomes cause for blame.

Denial, whether of reproach or conflict on the aggressor's part, paralyzes the victim, who cannot defend herself. Abuse is perpetrated by the refusal to acknowledge what is happening, discuss the situation, or jointly find solutions. If the conflict were out in the open, discussion would be possible and a solution might be forged. Within the scope of abusive communication, however, one must above all prevent the other person from thinking, understanding, or reacting. An effective way of aggravating the conflict is avoiding dialogue, which silently imputes blame on the other person. The victim is refused the right to be heard. Her version of the facts doesn't interest the abusive individual, who won't listen.

This refusal of dialogue is a way of saying, without directly expressing it in words, that the other person does not interest the aggressor or that she doesn't even exist. With anyone else one can ask questions if one doesn't understand, but with abusers discourse is tortuous and unclear and can only lead to mutual alienation. One is always on the farthest edge of comprehension.

When confronted with a refusal of direct verbal communication, it is not unusual for the victim to try written communication. She sends letters demanding explanations for what she perceives as her rejection; then, not receiving an answer, she writes again, this time searching for what in her behavior could elicit such an attitude. She'll even apologize for what she might have done to justify her aggressor's rejection.

These unanswered letters are sometimes used by the aggressor as a weapon against his target. In one example, after a violent scene in which the victim had reproached her husband for his lies and infidelities, her husband showed her letter in court, saying, "See, she recognizes her own violence!"

In certain instances when victims send registered letters in order to protect themselves, they are labeled litigious paranoids.

If there is an answer, it's usually indifferent and beside the point. In a letter full of emotion and affection, a wife writes to her husband: "Tell me, what is it in me that's so intolerable to make you hate me to such an extent that you can only show contempt for me and insult me? Why do you only talk in terms of reproach and blanket statements . . . ?" She obtains this clever answer, in a completely cold and unaffectionate tone of voice: "I'll explain. Facts don't exist. Everything can be reviewed. There are no frames of reference or obvious truths . . ."

Non-communication is found at every level of expression. The aggressor, confronted by his target, is tense, his body rigid and his look evasive: "From the time I first started at the company, my boss looked at me in a way that always made me feel uncomfortable, and I'd ask myself what I had done wrong."

DISTORTION OF LANGUAGE

In communicating with their victims, abusive individuals use a cold, flat tone of voice. It's a voice without affection that chills and disturbs, leaving traces of contempt and scorn in the most seemingly harmless remarks. The tone implies, even for neutral observers, innuendoes, unexpressed reproach, or veiled threats.

Anyone who has been the target of abusiveness right away recognizes that icy tone of voice that puts him on the alert and unleashes fear. The words are completely unimportant; it's the inherent threat that matters. Children who are victims of an emotionally abusive parent describe very well the change of tone just before aggression strikes: "Sometimes, at dinner, when he had just said something nice to one of my sisters, his voice became harsh, 'white.' I knew immediately that he would turn to me and that his words would hurt me."

Even during violent exchanges, the abuser's voice is never raised, leading the other person into a destabilized condition or one of nervous tension: "Most decidedly, you are simply an hysteric who shouts and cries all the time."

Very often the abusive individual doesn't make the effort to clearly articulate his remarks, or mutters something when the victim is in another room. This obliges her to move in order to hear what is being said or puts her in the position of asking to have it repeated. Then it's easy to say that she doesn't listen.

The message from someone abusive is deliberately blurred and imprecise in order to create confusion. He can answer, "I never said that" and avoid any blame. By means of allusion, he sends messages without compromising himself.

He is able to keep several different contradictory threads of conversation going, which ostensibly have no logical link.

He will also not finish sentences, opening the way for all kinds of misinterpretations and misunderstandings. Or he will transmit obscure messages and refuse to make them explicit. When a mother-in-law asks her son-in-law for some insignificant favor, the following exchange ensues:

"No, it's not possible."

"Why?"

"You should know."

"No, I don't understand!"

"Well, think about it."

His answers are offensive but said in a normal, calm, almost relaxed tone of voice. It is logical, when confronted by insinuations like these, to either look for what one has said or done wrong and blame oneself, or to get angry and start an argument. This strategy rarely fails, because guilt is hard to avoid, unless one is oneself perverse and abusive.

Destabilizing tactics are never obvious. A mother says to her daughter who is unsuccessfully trying to get pregnant, "Listen, I'll take care of my children as I please and you do the same with yours!" One might just imagine it as a simple oversight if it were followed by regrets or excuses. It's an example of a minor sting thrown here and there among others, with no attention paid to the other's soul.

Another verbal strategy commonly deployed by abusive individuals is the use of abstract, dogmatic, technical language to drag the other person into incomprehensible and uncharted territory where they don't dare ask for explanations for fear of looking like an idiot.

This cold, purely theoretical approach prevents the listener from thinking and therefore reacting. The abusive person, speaking in an authoritarian tone, gives an impression of knowledge, regardless of what he says. He impresses his audience with superficial erudition, using technical terms without caring about their meaning. The other will later say, "He bamboozled me; I don't know why I didn't react!"

To an abuser, what matters in conversation is the form and not the content; the appearance of knowledge will drown the fish. Answering his wife, who wanted to talk about their relationship, a husband takes this dogmatic tone: "You are introducing a questionable problem typical of castrating women, who project their phallic desire on men!"

These fierce, supposedly psychoanalytical interpretations succeed in disorienting the other, who is rarely able to turn the situation around to her advantage. Victims add that the abuser's arguments are often so incoherent that they should laugh, but that such random evil just makes them angry.

Another abusive procedure consists in spelling out the victims' intentions or guessing their secret thoughts, as if the aggressors know better than they what they are thinking: "I know very well that you hate the so-and-so's and that you're looking for a reason to avoid an encounter!"

LIES

Rather than using a direct lie, the abuser initially employs a mix of innuendo and unspoken hints to create a misunderstanding, which he will subsequently exploit to his advantage.

In his treatise *The Art of War*, composed in the fifth century B.C., the Chinese writer Sun Tsu taught that "the art of war is the art of trickery, always appearing the opposite of what one is, thereby increasing one's chances of victory."[1]

These incomplete, paradoxical messages correspond to a fear of the other's reaction. One articulates without being explicit, hoping the other person will understand. Most of the time these messages can only be decoded after the fact: a posteriori.

To speak without saying is a clever way of handling situations.

These indirect messages can seem general, even harmless, or obliquely aggressive: "Women are terrible!" "Working women certainly don't do much around the house!" which is immediately corrected if the partner protests: "I wasn't saying that about you. Heavens, you certainly can be sensitive!"

Having the upper hand in a verbal exchange is paramount, but an overtly direct approach would lead the partner to denounce the abuser's authoritarianism. These allusive techniques, on the contrary, destabilize and erode the other's identity, leading him or her to doubt the reality of what has occurred.

Another type of indirect lie consists in an imprecise or off-the-subject answer or diversionary attack. When a woman questions her husband's fidelity, his reply is, "In order for you to say something like that, you must have something to blame yourself for!"

Lies can also be part of the details: a husband answering his wife's accusation of having gone to the country for eight days with a girl says, "You're the liar. In the first place it was nine days, not eight, and secondly, it wasn't a girl but a woman!"

No matter what is said, abusers always find a way to be in the right, especially when the victim is already destabilized and, unlike her attacker, takes no pleasure in polemics. The unease induced in the victim is a result of the permanent confusion between truth and lies.

Lying in perverse and abusive narcissists becomes direct only during the destructive phase, as we shall see in the following chapter. At that point, lies fly in the face of any evidence. It is primarily a sincere lie that convinces the other. No matter how enormous the lie, the abuser persists and ultimately prevails.

Truth and lies have no meaning in abusive behavior: what is true is what the abuser is saying that very instant. These warped truths often approach a delirious construct. Every implicit message, even when clear, cannot be taken into consideration by the speaker. Since there is no outward trace of abuse, it doesn't actually exist. The lie simply corresponds to a need to ignore any blocking of his narcissistic interest.

These strategies illustrate how perverse abusers envelop themselves in a mysterious aura that wordlessly induces the other to believe in them: to hide in order to silently show.

THE USE OF SARCASM, RIDICULE, CONTEMPT

Contempt and ridicule are the message for outsiders—contempt toward the loathed partner, what he or she thinks and does, extending out to his or her circle. Contempt is the weapon of the weak and a protection against unwanted feelings. One hides behind a mask of irony or humor.

This ridicule and contempt are particularly directed against women. In the case of abusive sexuality, it's a denial of the woman's sex. Abusive narcissists deny the whole woman as an individual identity. They take pleasure in any kind of humor that ridicules women.

This attitude can be encouraged by the complacency of witnesses, as in the following example:

During a talk show on NBC, a young couple were to publicly debate the following problem: "He can't stand me because I'm not a top model." The young man explained that his girlfriend (the mother of his child) was not what he ultimately might have wished; she wasn't thin and sexy, her teeth and breasts were flawed, so therefore she wasn't desirable. His model of reference was Cindy Crawford. He was so scornful that his girlfriend burst into tears. He didn't show the slightest emotion and made no move to comfort her.

Members of the audience were supposed to give their opinion. Naturally, the women there protested against the man's attitude and some of them gave the young woman advice on how to improve her appearance, but most of the men just sat back, even joining in the criticism of the young woman's looks.

The program psychologist explained to the public that it only took one glance at Sherry to see that she didn't resemble Cindy Crawford, but that Bob had nevertheless loved her enough to want to have a baby with her. Yet nobody questioned the smugness of the spectators and organizers of the program, or the humiliation suffered by that woman.

Ridicule consists in mocking everything and everyone. This constant attitude diffuses suspicion—it's a relaxed way to behave—but creates a disagreeable atmosphere and shifts communication onto a deceitful, insincere plane.

Unkind remarks (hurtful truths) or slanderous remarks (lies) often spring from envy. Thus:

- A pretty girl who goes out with an older man is a whore.
- A demanding woman needs sex to put her in her place.
- A famous television newscaster obviously slept with everyone to get where she is.
- A colleague who succeeds owes it to the "casting couch."

It is basically women who are most often targeted in these attacks because of their sex.

The person who uses ridicule assumes a position of knowing. That gives him the right to make fun of someone or something, and he turns his audience into an ally.

The procedure can be direct: "But look here, didn't you know that . . . !" or indirect: "Didn't you see how she was . . . ?"

It's not unusual for the victim to completely swallow the abuser's criticism of her circle (of friends, coworkers, etc.) and ultimately believe the criticism justified.

Sarcasm and biting remarks are accepted as the price to pay for a relationship with a charming and seductive but difficult partner.

To keep his own head above water, the abuser needs to submerge the other. In order to accomplish this, he proceeds with tiny destabilizing moves, preferably in public; he'll begin with an innocuous, sometimes intimate incident exaggeratedly described, selecting an ally from the company.

Embarrassing the other becomes the goal. You sense the hostility but are unsure it's not humor. The abuser seems to tease, but in reality he is attacking weak points: a "big nose," "flat-chested," "difficulty in expressing oneself . . ."

The attack is made silently, through allusion and implication; one can hardly tell when it began or if it really is an attack. The aggressor never compromises himself, and often he'll turn the situation upside down by labeling his victim's aggressive desires: "If you think I'm stalking you, it's because you are actually the aggressor!"

As we have seen in clinical cases, a common abusive technique consists in saddling the other with a ridiculous nickname based on an oddity: Fatty, Mrs. Flabby, Big Slug. These nicknames, even when hurtful, are often accepted by an entourage that has become complacent and laughs.

All these disagreeable remarks create wounds that aren't compensated for by nice gestures. The resulting pain is ignored by the partner, who then turns it into ridicule.

There is also an element of gamesmanship in these verbal attacks, this mockery and cynicism: it's the pleasure of a quarrel and of pushing the other into opposition. The abusive nar-

cissist, as we have said, loves controversy. He is capable of espousing a point of view one day and defending its opposite the next just to reanimate the discussion or, deliberately, to shock. If the partner doesn't react sufficiently, all that's needed is a little more provocation. The partner who is a victim of this violence doesn't react because she is so accustomed to offering excuses for her abuser, but also because the violence has been established so insidiously. The sudden eruption of such a violent attitude would normally provoke anger, but because it's progressively set in place step by step, it defuses any reaction. The victim doesn't track the aggressiveness of the message until it's almost become a habit.

The conversation of the narcissistic abuser charms listeners who are unaware of the humiliation experienced by the victim. It is not unusual for the abuser to invite those close to the situation to participate willy-nilly in his demolition enterprise.

In short, to destabilize another person, one should:

· Mock their beliefs, political choices, likes
· No longer speak directly to them
· Make fun of them in public
· Tear them down in front of others
· Deny them any means of expression
· Tease them about their weaknesses
· Make unkind allusions, with no explanations
· Put in doubt and question all their judgmental and
  decision-making abilities

THE USE OF PARADOX

Sun Tsu also taught that to win a war, one must divide the enemy's army before the battle has even begun. "Try to win without going into battle. . . . Before fighting, they [the ancients] tried to weaken the enemy's confidence by humiliating and mortifying him and making his troops undergo difficult trials. Corrupt what is best around him with offers, promises, and presents, undermine confidence by forcing his star lieutenants into vile and shameful acts and be sure to divulge them."

During an emotionally abusive attack, there is an attempt to shake the other's foundations, to make her doubt her thoughts and feelings. The victim loses her sense of identity. She cannot think or comprehend. The goal is to deny her existence by paralyzing her and eroding her identity in order to prevent any emergence of conflict. One can attack without losing her altogether, but she remains at her abuser's disposal.

This is all accomplished by twin constraints: something is said verbally and its opposite is expressed non-verbally. The paradoxical message is composed of an explicit signal and an innuendo, which the abuser does not acknowledge. It's a highly effective way to destabilize the other.

One incarnation of the paradoxical message is the planting of doubt into more or less innocuous elements of daily life. The partner ends up shaken and no longer knows who's right and who's wrong. For example, it's enough to agree to a proposal suggested by the other, but, by adding a gesture, indicate that it's only for show.

A remark is made and immediately retracted but its traces remain, forming doubt: "Did he really mean or say that, or is it just me that misinterprets everything?" If the victim tries to express her doubt, she is branded a paranoid who gets it all wrong.

The paradox most often arises from a discrepancy between what is said and how it is said. This discrepancy misleads witnesses into a totally distorted grasp of the conversation.

It also consists in making the other feel tension and hostility without actually expressing it. This can involve indirect attacks where the abuser takes it out on objects. He'll slam doors, throw things, and then deny his aggressiveness.

A talk loaded with paradox confuses the other person. Because she is not very sure of her ground, she tends to exaggerate her feelings or justify herself.

Inconsistent messages are difficult to track. Their goal is to confuse and destabilize in order to maintain control by getting the victim mired in contradictory emotions and feelings. The abuser puts her in an impossibly awkward position and makes sure to always put her in the wrong. I have already said this but it can't be stressed enough: the aim of all these maneuvers is to control the feelings and the behavior of the other and even to see to it that they disqualify themselves, leaving the dominant position open for the abuser to fill.

Generally the partners of abusers, in a spirit of conciliation, choose to accept literally everything that is said, ignoring the contradictory non-verbal signals bombarding them: "When I threaten to walk out the door, my husband says he really cares about the relationship. Even if he wounds and humiliates me, there must be some truth in that."

Unlike in normal conflict, when dealing with an abusive narcissist, both true "fighting" and reconciliation are impossible. He never raises his voice, and only shows cold hostility, which he will deny if the question is raised. The other person becomes nervous and over-excited or bursts into tears. It's easy at that point to make fun of her anger and present the issue in a ridiculous light.

Even when fighting is ostensibly out in the open, the real subject of conflict is never really introduced because the victim doesn't know her ground. She feels permanently marginalized and stores up resentment. How can you label vague impressions, intuition, and emotions? Nothing is ever made concrete.

These destabilizing techniques, available to anyone but systematically used by an abuser, are never offset by excuses.

In blocking communication with contradictory messages, the abuser makes it impossible for the subject to respond appropriately because she doesn't understand the situation. She exhausts herself trying to find solutions, which are inadequate, in any case; eventually, no matter how strong she is, she cannot help feeling despair or depression.

This type of communication corresponds to an innate coherence in the relationship and, for a period of time, results in a kind of balance. Homeostasis forestalls anything that could break up the couple, allowing some stability to prevail in the painful relationship. In other situations, the victim has no choice but to submit.

Abusive communication is often made up of subtle messages that are not initially perceived as assaultive or destructive because other messages, simultaneously transmitted, scramble them. They are, very often, only decoded after the recipient is out from under the emotional abuse.

Only when she became an adult did she realize the ambiguity (double-meaning) of the postcards of nude women her stepfather sent her when she was a teenager. He wrote, "I think of you a lot!" At the time, she saw them as a mark of affection, but they made her angry. This realization allowed her to decode other messages from her stepfather that she hadn't understood then, but which had made her uncomfortable, like his looking at her breasts or telling dirty jokes.

This example of "incestuality" as defined by Racamier shows how fuzzy the boundary can be between moral and sexual abuse. In both cases, the other becomes an object. Brainwashing devalues and invalidates an individual but also affects others in the vicinity, who lose sight of who said and did what. In addition to the targeted person, who must be paralyzed into silence, the family, colleagues, and friends become totally confused.

The transference of guilt is another common element of abuse. The burden of guilt is entirely borne by the victim. This introjection of guilt becomes an "it's all my fault" syndrome and, for the emotional abuser, an external projection of his guilt in blaming the other: "It's all her fault!"

INVALIDATION

The erosion of identity involves stripping the other of any good qualities and repeatedly saying that they are worth nothing until finally they believe it.

We have already seen that this is accomplished by subterranean non-verbal communication strategies: scornful looks, "this-is-all-too-much" sighs, unsettling or spiteful implications, disagreeable and unkind remarks, and indirect criticism couched in the guise of humor.

Because these attacks are indirect, it is virtually impossible to see them clearly for what they are, and therefore to defend oneself. When these words resonate in a fragile identity and a person lacking self-confidence or are addressed to a child, they are incorporated by the victim, who accepts them as the truth. "You're not capable of accomplishing anything." "No one would have anything to do with you if I weren't around—you'd be all alone without me!" The abuser sweeps his victim along and imposes upon her his falsified vision of reality.

Once victims hear, directly or indirectly, that they are worthless, their identity erodes and they become effectively null. The concept can't be properly examined and their identity disappears because the other person has stated that as fact.

Invalidation and erosion of identity using paradox, lies, and other procedures fan out from the designated target to include her family and her circle of friends and acquaintances: "She only knows a bunch of jerks!"

All these strategies are designed to make the other person sink deeper into a condition of non-identity, while heightening the abuser's self-esteem.

DIVIDE AND CONQUER

Sun Tsu also says: "Trouble your adversary's governments, sow dissension among his leaders by inciting jealousy and distrust, provoke undiscipline, furnish causes for discontent. . . . Division unto death is our goal, which we will try to attain by discrediting and throwing suspicion on the Sovereign's generals until the gossip reaches his inner sanctum."

The abusive narcissist excels in the art of pitting people against each other and provoking jealousies and rivalries. It can be done allusively, in the following manners: (1) By insinuating doubt: "Don't you find that the so-and-so's are thus and such?" (2) By revealing what one person says about another: "Your brother told me he thought you behaved badly," or (3) By lying to incite people to become adversarial.

The greatest pleasure for an abuser lies in the destruction of one individual by another and watching the battle from which both will emerge weakened; this result will ultimately reinforce his omnipotence.

In the workplace this is translated into gossip, innuendoes, or privileges granted to one employee over another and mercurial preferential treatment. It also gives rise to rumors that will intangibly hurt the victim, who is unable to trace their origins.

In a relationship, cultivating doubt and jealousy by allusions and implications is an effective way of tormenting and keeping the partner dependent.

Shakespeare's *Othello* is all about provoking jealousy in another person. In the play, Othello, not jealous by nature, is described as noble, generous, and disinclined to believe in the existence of evil. He is not vindictive or even violent. He becomes jealous because of Iago's clever maneuvers. He has great faith in his wife, just as he has faith in Iago, and initially he can't conceive that his wife could be unfaithful. In his famous "Credo," Iago declares that he likes to do evil for the love of evil. Later he admits he is shocked by the "daily beauty" of an upstanding man like Cassio and the purity of Desdemona, and induced to destroy that virtue and that purity. Iago delights in vileness and weaving intrigue.

Provoking jealousy is also a way for the abuser to stay above it all, above anger and hate. It's what happens between the partner and his rival. He keeps score and doesn't "dirty his hands." By making the other jealous, the abuser, who is basically envious, brings his rival down to his level, insinuating that "you and I are alike!"

The victim doesn't dare to directly attack her abuser. She avoids confrontation by becoming jealous and continues to protect the abuser. It's easier to deal with the third party that the abuser dangles as prey.

THE IMPOSITION OF POWER

The logic of abusive power decrees that the stronger person subjects the weaker. Power is grasped with words: to give the impression of knowing better and possessing a truth: *the* truth. The abuser's conversation sums up declared assertions that seem universally true. The abuser "knows" he's right and tries to convert the other by forcing her to accept his statements. For example, instead of saying, "I don't like so-and-so," he says: "So-and-so is a jerk. Everybody knows it and even you can't disagree!"

He then proceeds to generalize and turn his remark into a universal premise. The listener says to herself: "He must be right; he seems to know what he's talking about." Narcissistic abusers attract partners who are unsure of themselves and tend to think that others know better; they are, in fact, very reassuring for their more fragile partners.

This kind of self-conceit, where everything is played out beforehand, is not far from a paranoid mind-set. A paranoid must uncover a negative side in everyone, even if the motives for his disparagement are slippery. They are sometimes linked to an opening or weakness in the other but more often they are left to outside circumstances.

The process of domination is gradually established: the victim submits and is then subjugated and controlled; her identity erodes. If she should rebel, her aggressiveness and maliciousness are pinpointed. In any case, a blitzkrieg operation is deployed based on fear and aimed at total obedience. The other must act according to the abuser's standards and think as he sees fit. Any critical sense is impossible. The other exists only to the degree that she acts out her assigned role. It's a matter of eroding her identity, annihilating her, and denying any differences between abuser and victim.

The aggressor uses this power for his own benefit and to the detriment of the other's interests. The relationship of the victim to her abuser becomes dependent, a dependence attributed to the victim but projected by the instigator. Every time the abuser consciously expresses his need for dependence he makes sure that it remains ungratified: either the demands exceed the other's capabilities and the narcissist points out her helplessness or the demand is made when it can't be answered. He solicits rejection because it reassures him to prove that life is exactly as he suspected.

Emotional abuse differs from abuse of power or tyranny. Tyranny is a way of gaining power by force. The oppression is obvious. One submits because the other clearly holds the power. In the case of direct abuse of power, the goal is simply to dominate.

An example of the latter is given by Einstein who, exasperated by the presence of his wife and two children and reluctant to initiate a break, writes down draconian and humiliating conditions for their life together:

A. You will see that:
   1) My underwear and sheets are kept in order
   2) I will be served three meals a day in my office
   3) My bedroom and office will always be well maintained and my worktable left untouched by anyone but me
B. You will renounce any personal relationship with me, except when necessary to keep up appearances.
   In particular, you will not demand that:
   1) I sit with you at home
   2) I travel with you
C. You will explicitly promise to obey the following stipulations:
   1) You will not expect any affection from me and you will not reproach me for it
   2) You will answer immediately when I speak to you
   3) You will leave my room and office immediately and without protests when I should so ask
   4) You will promise not to disparage me, with words or deeds, in the eyes of my children[2]

Here abuse of power is clear and even written down. In an abuser's case, domination is underhanded and denied, often beneath a mask of gentleness and benevolence. The partner is not conscious of the violence and sometimes even thinks she's in control. There is never outspoken conflict. If the violence is carried out under the surface, it's because of the very real warped relationship between the abuser and his victim.

CHAPTER FIVE

THE STAGES OF EMOTIONAL ABUSE

T o resist control means to expose oneself to hate. At this stage, the other, who had only existed as a useful object, becomes a dangerous other one who must be eliminated by whatever means. The abusive strategy now becomes clear.

HATRED BECOMES OVERT

The hatred phase emerges clearly when the victim reacts, attempting to recover her identity and regain a little freedom. Something is triggered inside her and makes her say, "That's enough," either because an outside factor has made her conscious of her enslavement (sometimes after she has witnessed her aggressor attack someone else) or because the abuser has found another potential partner and tries to push aside "the incumbent" by increasing the violence.

At the moment the victim seems about to escape, the attacker experiences panic and fury—and he explodes.

The victim must be silenced when she expresses herself.

This is an extremely violent phase of pure hatred, full of low blows, demeaning insults, and humiliations; every characteristic of the other is made fun of and mocked. This armor of sarcasm protects the abuser against what he most fears: communication.

In her concern to connect, the other exposes herself. The more she exposes herself, the more she is attacked and the more she suffers. The sight of this suffering is insupportable to the abuser, who steps up his attacks in order to silence the victim. When the other reveals her weaknesses, they are immediately turned against her.

The hatred already existed during the ascendance phase, but was diverted and masked to keep the relationship static. What was always there underground now becomes apparent. The demolition project is systemized.

Contrary to general belief, this is not love alchemized into hatred, but envy transformed into hate. Nor is it love-hate, because the abuser never really loved in the true sense. One might even, after Maurice Hurni and Giovanna Stoll,[1] describe the abusive relationship as a hatred of love. First, it's non-love parading as desire, not for the person herself, but for what she has that the abuser wishes to appropriate. Second, it's a hidden hatred, linked to the frustration of not obtaining from the other all that one might have wished. When the hatred is frankly expressed, it comes with a desire to destroy and annihilate the other's identity. Even with time, the abuser can't renounce this hatred. It's clear to him, "Because that's the way it is!" even though his motive may be a mystery to others.

He justifies this hatred by blaming it on *his* persecution by the victim, which legitimizes his defense. As with paranoid patients, he is now haunted by a persecution complex: he anticipates defense mechanisms that will lead to malicious and offensive conduct. Anything that goes wrong is the fault of others who are in league against him.

The abuser's hatred is a function of projecting the degree of hatred he *imagines* the victim bears against him. He sees her as a destructive, violent, deadly monster. In reality, the victim during this phase feels neither hatred nor anger, which would at least shield her and allow her to defend herself. The aggressor ascribes to her the most evil intentions and anticipates her actions by attacking first. The victim is permanently guilty of offensive intentions.

This hatred, projected onto someone else, provides the abuser with a defense against what could be more serious psychotic symptoms. It's also a way, while establishing a new relationship, to defend himself against any unconscious hate he may harbor toward the most recent partner. By focusing the hate on her predecessor, one can ascribe every virtue to the new partner. When the "hated" victim realizes that she is a sacrificial pawn in reinforcing the latest relationship, she feels trapped and manipulated yet again.

The world of the narcissistic abuser is divided into good and bad and it's no good being on the bad side. Separation and distance do nothing to mitigate the hate.

During this process, each individual fears the other: the aggressor is scared of the omnipotence he attributes to his victim; the victim is scared of the aggressor's psychological, and sometimes physical, violence.

ABUSE COMES INTO PLAY

This is a cold, verbal violence composed of disparagement, implied hostility, and condescending and wounding insults. The destructive effects come from seemingly harmless but continuous attacks that one knows will never stop. Every insult echoes previous ones, which makes it impossible to forget; the victim wants only to forget, but the attacker refuses to allow this.

On the surface, ones sees nothing or next to nothing, but a cataclysm will implode families, institutions, or individuals. The violence, rarely physical, usually follows an overly sharp reaction on the victim's part. This makes it the perfect crime.

The threats are always indirect and veiled: one makes sure the victim knows, via mutual friends or the children (themselves manipulated), the consequence of not following the partner's wishes. One sends letters or makes telephone calls that are often described as land mines or time bombs.

When real physical violence (sometimes culminating in murder) is added to the subterranean violence we've described (blackmail, intimidation, veiled threats), it represents a derailment of the abuser's plans because he would prefer to kill indirectly or, more precisely, induce the other to kill herself.

Marks of hostility don't show up during moments of crisis or over-excitement, but they are constantly there, slowly stalking the victim's soul every day or several times a week for months, even years. They are not expressed in anger but in an icy tone, stating a truth or an evident fact. An abuser knows how to mete out his violence and just how far he can go. He backtracks if he senses his opponent reacting. The attacks are distilled into tiny doses when there are witnesses. When the victim does fall into the "provocation" trap by raising her voice, she's the one who seems aggressive while her aggressor can pose as the victim.

The innuendoes often refer to incidents the two share that only the victim can spot. It's not unusual that judges, called upon to make sense of these complicated divorce cases, should be troubled and even manipulated despite their innate suspicion and efforts to take every precaution.

Professor Emil Coccaro, in a study on the biology of aggressiveness, has called this "predatory aggression." Individuals
choose their victims and premeditate their attack in the same
way a predatory animal stalks its prey. Abuse becomes the
means that allow the attacker to obtain what he wants.

The violence is also asymmetrical. In the case of symmetri-
cal violence, both adversaries accept confrontation and doing
battle. Here, on the contrary, the person unleashing the violence considers himself existentially superior to his victim, a
definition generally accepted by that victim. This type of insidious violence has been called "punitive violence" by Reynaldo
Perrone.[2] With these examples, there is no let-up or reconciliation, making the violence pent-up and concealed. Neither
of the players in this melodrama discusses it with the outside
world. The dispenser of violence believes his victim deserves
what she's getting and has no right to complain. If she reacts
and stops behaving like a docile "thing," she is considered
threatening or aggressive. The instigator becomes victim. Every emotional or wounded reaction brings on heightened violence or a diversionary maneuver (indifference, fake surprise,
etc.).

A reciprocal phobic process has been set in place: the abuser
feels icy rage at the mere sight of the victim; the mere sight of
her tormentor unleashes horrible fear in the victim.

The abuser never lets go of his designated prey. He frequently avows his determination openly: "As of now, my only
goal in life will be to prevent her from living." He then makes
sure that this becomes true.

Once set in motion, this vicious circle is impossible to stop
because the pathology of both attacker and victim grows: the
abuser becomes more and more violent and humiliating while
the victim is more and more powerless and damaged. Nothing

can actually prove the reality of what's happening. Physical violence can be testified to by outside evidence: eyewitnesses, police and medical reports. With emotional abuse, there is no proof. It's a clean violence. Nobody sees anything.

THE VICTIM IS CORNERED

During the ascendancy of the control phase, the emotional abuser essentially acted to inhibit his victim's powers of reasoning and critical judgment. In the next phase, through a strategic series of commands, he provokes feelings, acts, and reactions.

If the opponent can "outdo" his rival in abusive defense strategies, the battle can only end in the surrender of the less perverse of the two.

The abuser tries to makes the victim act against him so he can denounce her as "evil." What's crucial is that she seem responsible for what has happened. He uses a weakness—a depressive, hysterical, or temperamental tendency—overexaggerates this trait, and then leads the victim on to discredit herself. Pushing the other into making mistakes allows the abuser to criticize and tear her down, but even more, reinforces her poor self-image and guilt.

When the victim loses control, the abuser simply injects a small dose of provocation and contempt to obtain a reaction, and later reproaches her for it. If, for example, the reaction is anger, he makes sure that everyone sees it. On occasion, an outsider might even feel compelled to call the police. One even sees cases of abusers egging their victims on: "Poor thing, you can't expect anything from life; I don't know why you haven't jumped out the window!" It's easy after that for the abuser to make the victim a mental case.

The victim needs to act, but because she is blocked by the

hold over her, she can only find her freedom in an extreme gesture. To an outsider, any impulsive action, especially a violent one, is considered pathological. The person reacting to provocation seems responsible for the crisis. Guilty in the eyes of the abuser, she appears like the aggressor to outsiders, who don't understand that she can no longer live trapped in a horrible situation. Whatever she does, she can't set herself free: if she reacts, she is responsible for starting the conflict, and if she doesn't react, the deadly stalking of her soul continues.

As he drives his victim to destruction, the abuser gets that much more pleasure from pointing out her weaknesses or unleashing her violence. He makes her feel debased and unworthy. Depending on her reaction, she is described as temperamental and neurotic, alcoholic, or suicidal. The victim feels defenseless and tries to justify herself as if she were, in fact, guilty. The abuser's pleasure doubles: he bamboozles or humiliates his victim and subsequently rubs her nose in her humiliation.

While the victim dwells on her guilt, the abuser benefits from the situation, making sure to cast himself as the victim.

Justification becomes impossible when nothing is said and no reproach is made. Desperate to find a solution to this horrifying impasse, the victim may be tempted in turn to use innuendo and manipulation. The relationship then becomes ambiguous: who is the abuser and who the victim?

The ideal outcome for the abuser is to succeed in making the other "evil," which transforms the evil into something more normal because it is now shared. He wants to inject the other with what is bad in him. To corrupt is the ultimate goal. His greatest satisfaction lies in driving his target to destructive acts or, in a larger framework, leading several individuals to finish each other off.

All abusers, sexual or emotional, try to drag others into

their orbit and distort the rules. Their destructive capability depends on the propaganda they disseminate among victims' families, friends, and associates, showing to what extent the victims are "evil" and that it is therefore normal to blame them. Sometimes they succeed and seduce allies by ridiculing and scorning moral values. Not leading others into a circle of violence means failure for abusers and, therefore, becomes the only way to stop the spread of the abusive process.

CHAPTER SIX

THE ABUSER

A busive strategies may be used as self-defense by any person in a crisis. Narcissistic personality traits are common enough (egocentricity, need for admiration, intolerance of criticism), but they are not necessarily pathological. Besides, every one of us has probably at one time or another manipulated someone else to gain the upper hand, just as we have all felt a passing destructive hatred. What distinguishes us from abusive individuals is the impermanence of this behavior and our feelings, which are followed by remorse and regret. A neurotic lives on internal conflict. The concept of perverse abuser implies a strategy of using and then destroying another human being without guilt.

Many psychoanalysts claim we all have a bit of the perverse in us that allows us to defend ourselves, but a perverse narcissist only functions by gratifying his destructive impulses.

ABUSIVE NARCISSISM

The word perversion (from the Latin *per-vertere*: return, reverse) first appeared in the French language in 1444 and meant the transformation from good to evil. Today, its accepted definition implies moral judgment.

In the nineteenth century, alienist doctors sought to establish non-responsibility for perverse individuals on a medical-legal plane without labeling them insane. They defined perverseness as instinctual deviation, both social and moral.

Pinel in 1809 regrouped under the label "mania without delirium" any pathology related to the plurality of instincts: perversion, asocial behavior, pyromania, kleptomania, etc.

Still later, Krafft-Ebing centered the definition around sexual perversion.

The term narcissism as related to homosexuality appears in Freud for the first time in 1910. He subsequently distinguishes primary from secondary narcissism. The idea of primary narcissism is subject to many variations in psychoanalytical literature.[1]

The ambiguity attached to the adjective "perverse" corresponds to two nouns: *perversity* and *perversion*. From a psychoanalytic viewpoint, perversion is a deviation from the standard sexual act (defined as coitus seeking orgasm from vaginal penetration), while perversity suggests cruelty or specific maliciousness in the character and behavior of certain individuals. Bergeret[2] differentiates between perversion of character (i.e., individuals suffering from perversity) and sexual perversion.

The psychoanalyst P. C. Racamier[3] is one of the first to elaborate on the concept of perverse narcissist. Among others, Alberto Einguer[4] tried to define it as follows: "Perverse narcissistic individuals are those who, under the influence of their grandiose self, try to create a bond with a second individual, specifically attacking the narcissistic integrity of the other with the goal of disarming him/her. They also attack their love of self, their self-confidence, their self-esteem, and their belief in themselves. They seek, at the same time, to make the other believe that his/her dependence on them is sought desperately and is irreplaceable."

Abusive narcissists are considered asymptomatic psychotics who find their equilibrium by discharging onto another person the pain they can't feel and the internal conflicts they refuse to acknowledge. They do wrong because they can't exist any other way. They themselves were hurt during childhood and, in turn, this is how they try to survive. This transference of pain at the expense of another permits them to attain self-confidence and self-esteem.

NARCISSISM

The dysfunctional behaviors of a narcissistic personality display at least five of the following symptoms:

- A grandiose sense of his/her importance
- Fantasies of unlimited success/power
- Thoughts of being unique and "special"
- Belief that everything is owed to him/her
- Exploitation of others in relationships
- Lack of empathy

Otto Kernberg's description of pathological narcissism (1975) is very close to our present-day definition:

The principal characteristics of these narcissistic personalities are a sense of grandiosity, extreme egocentricity, a total lack of empathy for others, although they crave admiration and approval. These patients feel intense envy of those who seem to possess things they don't have or who simply find pleasure in living. Not only do they lack deep affective feelings and are incapable of understanding others' complex emotions, but their own emotions are mono-dimensional and flare up only to rapidly die out. In particular, they don't suffer true feelings of sadness, loss, and mourning; this inability to experience depressive reactions is a basic element of their personality. If they are abandoned or disappointed, they can seem depressed, but upon closer examination it's more a question of anger or resentment combined with a desire for revenge than deep sadness for the loss of a person they valued.[5]

A Narcissus, such as Ovid's Narcissus,[6] is someone who thinks he has found himself by looking in the mirror. His life consists in searching for his reflection in the gaze of others. The other exists, not as an individual, but as a mirror. A Narcissus is an empty shell with no real existence; he is a "pseudo" person who creates illusions in order to mask his emptiness. His fate is an attempt to avoid death because he has never recognized himself as an individual and has been obliged to construct a game of mirrors to give himself the illusion of existing. Even if, like a kaleidoscope, the game repeats and multiplies itself, the foundation of his individuality rests on a void.

THE TRANSITION TO ABUSIVENESS

This soulless Narcissus will attach himself to the other and, leechlike, try to inhale his or her life's blood. Because he is incapable of a true relationship, he can only do it in an abusive framework of destructive evil. Abusive human beings unquestionably experience extreme and fundamental delight in the doubts and suffering of others; they also take pleasure in subjugating and humiliating them.

The root of the process begins with creating an empty self out of mirror images, just as a robot is built to imitate life and seem human.

Sexual aberration and evil are the inevitable results of this empty construct. Like a vampire, the narcissist needs nourishment from another substance. When life does not exist, one attempts to appropriate it or, failing that, to destroy it so there will be no life anywhere. An insubstantial reflection lives inside abusers and a victim is only another reflection, not a real human being. Any situation that calls into question this mirror construct, masking a voice, will unleash a chain reaction of destructive fury. Abusive narcissists are reflective machines that look in vain for their image in other people's mirrors. They are insensitive and unfeeling. How can a machine be sensitive? This way they won't suffer. Suffering presupposes human flesh and existence. Only those human beings who are present in the world can have a history.

A fresh start might be possible for abusive narcissists if they become aware of their suffering. It would signify something else altogether and the end of their previous conduct.

MEGALOMANIA

Abusive narcissists are megalomaniacs who judge the standards of what is good and bad and what is the truth. They are often viewed as moralizing, distant, and superior. Other people feel guilty even when they don't say a word. Abusers seem to adopt irreproachable values, which on the one hand deceives others and, on the other, creates a favorable self-image. They denounce human evil.

They want people to be interested in them, but show a total lack of interest and empathy toward others. They are "owed."

They criticize everyone, never acknowledging the slightest mistake or blame on their part. Faced with an all-powerful and righteous adversary, the victim becomes weak and liable to fault and error. To invalidate others is a way of not seeing one-self and also of defending oneself against suffering a severe and disabling order.

Abusers enter into a relationship in order to seduce. They are often described as brilliant, charming, and seductive. Once the fish is caught, it has to be kept on the hook as long as it's needed. Another is not seen or heard and exists only to serve a need. In the abuser's world of logic, there is no place for respect of another individual. Seduction leading to abuse does not permit feelings of any kind because the underlying principle of abusive behavior is avoidance of emotion. The goal becomes "no surprises." Abusers are uninterested in the complex emotions of others. They are impervious to other individuals and what makes them separate and different entities, unless they feel that this difference has the potential to unsettle them. They totally deny the other's identity because their views and sensibilities must conform to the abuser's image of the world.

The strength of abusers lies in their insensitivity. They don't know what moral scruples are; therefore they don't have a guilty conscience and never suffer. They can attack with impunity because even if the partners try to defend themselves, they were chosen for their inherent vulnerability.

Abusers can become passionate about a person, an activity, or an idea, but these passions are only superficial. They are unaware of real emotion, particularly feelings of sadness or mourning. Disappointments cause anger or resentment, along with the desire for revenge. This explains the destructive rage that takes hold of them after a separation. When an abuser perceives a narcissistic hurt (defeat, rejection), he feels an uncontrolled desire for revenge. In a quick-tempered person, anger quickly dissipates, but in the abuser an unyielding bitterness takes root that he will play out to the greatest possible extent.

Perverse abusers, like all paranoid types, maintain sufficient emotional distance to never truly engage in a relationship. The effectiveness of their attacks comes from the fact that neither the victim nor an outside observer can possibly imagine such a lack of caring and compassion toward the suffering of another human being.

VAMPIRISM

The partner doesn't exist as a person but as a prop for a quality the abuser wishes to appropriate. Abusers receive nourishment from the life energy of those who fall under their spell. By invading the psychic space of the other, they try to take possession of this gratifying sustenance.

The problem for the narcissistic abuser lies in finding a remedy to fill his emptiness. In order not to face this void (which might initiate a cure), the narcissist projects himself onto his opposite. He becomes perverse in the basic sense of the term: he turns away from the void inside him (the non-perverse person) and confronts it. From this avoidance springs his love/hate for a material personality that is the most explicit symbol of our interior life. The narcissist needs to fill himself with the flesh and essence of another. But still he cannot find nourishment because nothing exists within that allows him to hold and make another's substance his own. Therefore, substantiality becomes a dangerous enemy because it reveals the void within.

Abusive narcissists intensely envy those who seem to possess what they do not or who simply enjoy life. The act of appropriation can take place in a social framework: seducing a partner, for example, who is able to ease introductions into artistic or intellectual circles that one wants access to. Having a partner with conduits to power is certainly a benefit. Next, they attack the other's self-esteem and self-confidence in order to increase their own worth. They appropriate the other's sense of self.

Because of their early childhood history, abusive narcissists have not matured and come into their own and they jealously observe those who have. Faced with their own emptiness, they try to destroy the happiness around them. Prisoners of their own inflexible defense system, they can't bear to see freedom in others. Unable to physically let go and enjoy themselves, they attempt to prevent others, even their own children, from natural pleasures. They undermine simple relationships because of cynicism and their incapacity to love. Abusive narcissists need to triumph over and annihilate someone else in order to feel superior and accept themselves. They must destroy to find affirmation.

Their critical sense is highly developed, so they spend a lot of time criticizing everyone and everything; this allows them to remain all-powerful: "If others are worthless, that means I must be better than they are."

Their driving force is envy and their objective is taking over.

To envy is to covet and to feel spiteful irritation at the sight of the happiness and the advantages of other people. From the beginning, we are dealing with an abusive mentality based on a perception of what the other possesses and they lack. It's naturally a subjective perception that can occasionally become frenzied. The envy has two characteristics: egocentricity on the one hand, and malevolence, accompanied by a desire to harm the envied person, on the other. This presupposes a feeling of inferiority vis-à-vis that person, who possesses what one covets. The envious one is sick to see the other with material or spiritual benefits, but he is more anxious to destroy than to acquire them. If they were his, he hasn't the resources to know what to do with them. Humiliating and disparaging the other suffices to make up the difference separating the two and the envied object will therefore assume demon-like features.

What abusers envy the most is the other's life. Since they aren't any happier with others than they are with themselves, envying another's success forces them to confront their own feelings of failure. They impose on others their dark vision of the world and their chronic dissatisfaction with life. They dampen the enthusiasm of the people around them, seeking foremost to show that the world and its inhabitants are evil and that their partner is also bad. They drag the other down with their pessimism into a depressed state, only to reproach them for it later.

Their deficiencies are shown up by the desires and vitality of the other; here we find the longing, common to so many of us, for the special bond between mother and child. This is why abusers often choose as their victims people full of energy and love of life, just as they seek to secure their own strength. Their appropriateness is made real by the enslavement and subjugation of the victim, who has become dependent and easily manipulated.

Appropriation is the logical sequel to envy. The benefits in question are rarely material. They are elusive spiritual and moral qualities that can't be stolen, such as love of life, sensitivity, creativity, charm, or musical and literary gifts. Things happen so that when the partner presents an idea, it doesn't remain his but is immediately taken over by an abuser. In a give-and-take relationship, one not blinded by hate and envy, the abuser might learn how to acquire these qualities, but that presupposes a modesty he doesn't have.

Emotional abusers sometimes appropriate the passions of the other because they care passionately about the other. But more often, they get interested in the other because he or she possesses something the abusers themselves might care about passionately. One sees in abusers wild infatuations followed by brutal and irreparable rejection. People around them don't understand how someone can fall from grace in the blink of an eye for no apparent reason. Emotional abusers absorb positive energy from those closest to them, which nourishes and regenerates them, only to subsequently unload all their negative energy on those same people.

The victim brings an enormous amount to the table, but it's never enough. Emotional abusers, never actually happy, always victimize themselves and always blame mother (or the object of the maternal transference). Abusers attack in order to escape the victimization they have borne since childhood. In a relationship, this "I am a victim" attitude seduces a partner who wants to console and heal before putting them at fault. Abusers often pose as abandoned victims after a separation, which then allows them to seduce their next partner: another healer.

DENIAL OF RESPONSIBILITY

Because they have no real subjectivity, abusers consider themselves not responsible. They are as absent to others as they are to themselves. You can't count on them or grasp them because, as Gertrude Stein said, "There's no there, there." When they blame others for what happens to them, they aren't accusing but stating a simple fact: since they *can't* be responsible, someone else must be. Blaming someone else and making them seem bad frees and exonerates the abuser. Everything that goes wrong is always someone else's fault: the abuser is never responsible and never guilty.

Abusers deploy an arsenal of defense mechanisms to protect themselves: never come forward and always blame others for any difficulties or failures. A constant denial of reality, down to minute incidents of daily life and when faced with evidence to the contrary, is another useful ploy. Suffering and doubt are equally excluded and must be borne by others. Stalking and attacking others is a means of avoiding pain, sadness, and depression. Emotional abusers have difficulty making decisions in daily life and need to have others assume the responsibility. Because they are not completely autonomous and are dependent on others, they stick close to people and fear separation; nonetheless, they believe it is the other who asks for subjection. They refuse to acknowledge the devouring nature of their "clinging" behavior, which could lead to a negative perception of their own image. This explains their abusive conduct toward an overly kind and solicitous partner. If, however, this same partner should become independent, he or she is perceived as hostile and rejecting.

When alone, they feel ill at ease or powerless and desperately seek to obtain the support and help of others. They are equally incapable of initiating projects and acting on their own. They solicit rejection because this confirms their predictions about life, but when a relationship ends, they urgently look for another who will assure them of the support they desperately need.

PARANOIA

Emotional abusers tend to appear moralizing: they give lessons in honesty and integrity to other people. This characteristic resembles a paranoid personality. A paranoid personality is defined by:

- Hypertrophy of the self: pride and feelings of superiority
- Psychorigidity: obstinacy, intolerance, cold rationality, difficulty in showing positive emotions, scorn for others

- Suspicion: exaggerated fear of aggressiveness in others, feelings of being victimized by the ill-will of another, jealousy
- Wrong judgments: interpreting neutral events as being directed at them

However, unlike the paranoid personality, the emotional abuser is familiar with the rules and regulations of life in society and gleefully distorts them to his advantage. It's in his nature to challenge the laws. The goal is to confuse his antagonist by proving that his value system doesn't work and leading him toward a perverse morality.

Paranoid personalities seize power by force while emotional abusers seduce—although when that no longer works, they can resort to violence. This violent phase is itself a process of paranoid decompensation: the other must be destroyed because he is dangerous, and one must attack first.

As we have noted, abusive narcissism is a means of avoiding anguish by projecting everything bad outside. It is a defense against psychological disintegration. By attacking others, abusers seek protection. Psychological pain replaces any semblance of guilt and is violently transferred onto the scapegoat, who becomes the receptacle of everything his or her aggressor cannot bear. Abusers continue to function in a fragmented manner because, since childhood, they have learned to separate out the healthy from the wounded parts of their psyche in order to protect themselves. Their world is divided into good and bad. Projecting what is bad onto someone else allows them to feel better about themselves and guarantees them relative stability. Because they feel impotent, abusers fear the power they imagine others to have. They ascribe to them, in an almost delirious and crazy sense, a malice that is only a projection of their own malevolence.

When this strategy works, with the hatred projected onto a target (that soon becomes prey), it calms inner tension; this allows the emotional abuser to act pleasantly in the outside world. This explains the astonishment, or even denial, of people who learn about the abusive actions of a close relation who had previously only shown his or her positive aspect. The evidence of the victims, seen in this light, hardly seems credible.

CHAPTER SEVEN

THE VICTIM

THE VICTIM AS OBJECT

The victim is a victim because he or she has been chosen by the abuser. He or she becomes the scapegoat who is responsible for everything bad. From now on, he or she will be the object of violence, sparing the attacker doubt or depression.

The victim is innocent of the crime for which he or she will pay. However, even witnesses to the abuse suspect the victim. It all takes place as if an innocent could not exist. People imagine that the victim either tacitly agrees or is an accomplice, conscious or unconscious, to the abuse.

According to René Girard,[1] group rivalry in primitive societies produced situations of indiscriminate violence that spread through mimicry and were only resolved by a human sacrifice of the person (or group of persons) named as responsible for the violence. The death of the scapegoat led to a purging of the violence and the propitiation of the victim. Today, victims are not sacrificed, but instead of being considered innocent, they are simply considered weak. It's common to hear it said of a person who has been victimized that they were predisposed to the condition, because of either weakness or character deficiencies. We will see, on the contrary, that victims are generally chosen for the positive qualities they have, which the abuser then seeks to appropriate.

Why is the victim chosen?

Because she is there, and for an unspecified reason becomes troublesome. The victim is an interchangeable object who happens to be there at the right/wrong time and makes the mistake of letting herself be seduced and, sometimes, of seeing too clearly. She is only of interest to the seducer when she can be used or seduced. She becomes an object of hate as soon as she tries to work her way free or has nothing left to give.

It's not important who she is, since she is only a "thing." Nonetheless, the abuser carefully avoids pitting himself against other narcissistic abusers or paranoid personalities who are too much like him. When these two groups come together, the annihilating effect on the victim increases dramatically. One sees this particularly in groups and organizations. How much more amusing to despise or mock someone in front of an encouraging onlooker. It's not unusual for abusers to get tacit approval from witnesses who, while not actual accomplices, become destabilized and then more or less won over.

The nature of an abusive attack lies in aiming at the other's vulnerability, where weakness or pathology exists. Every individual exposes a weak point that the abuser will hammer away at. Just as a climber hooks onto the fault in the mountainside, so an abuser uses the other's faults. An abuser shows tremendous intuition about where the weaknesses lie, finding how best to hurt and wound. In some cases, the fault can be exactly the one a victim refuses to acknowledge in herself, and the abusive attack becomes a painful revelation. It can also be a symptom that the victim has tried to minimize or regularize, which the abusive attack reactivates.

Abusive violence confronts the victim with her fault and/ or forgotten childhood traumas. It stirs up the death impulse that lies quiescent in each one of us. Abusers root out the self-destructive seed that destabilizing communication with the victim will activate. Relationships with abusers function as negative mirror images. A positive self-image is transformed into non-love.

To label the victim accomplice to her abuser makes no sense to the extent that the victim, once the hold over her occurs, does not have the psychological means to behave otherwise: she is paralyzed. The fact that she participates passively does not make her less of a victim.

A victim speaks: "If I've lived with a man who didn't love me, I'm partially responsible; if I didn't see anything when I was cheated on, that's linked to my history; later, though, the way the separation played itself out was totally unpredictable and it was impossible to adapt. Even if I now understand that the behavior and mental attitude weren't personal, I consider it a horrible attack on my soul and attempted psychological murder."

The victim is neither a masochist nor a depressive person, but the abuser will manipulate the depressed or masochistic tendency in her.

How do we differentiate between masochistic complaisance and the deep depression of an abuser's victim?

THE VICTIM AS MASOCHIST?

What surprises one from the very first is the victims' acceptance of their condition.

We have seen that an abuser's language is completely one way, denying the other's subjectivity. We can even ask why his word is accepted and even internalized by the victims. Why do the victims continue their deference even when reality belies the language? We have indicated that they are psychologically bound. Being a useful pawn isn't necessarily the game they would like to have played.

Freud distinguished three forms of masochism: erogenous, feminine, and moral.[2] Moral masochism consists in a proactive search for failure and suffering in order to gratify a need for punishment. According to Freudian criteria, the masochistic personality not only relishes the suffering, tensions, and complications of existence, but never fails to complain and seem pessimistic. His clumsy behavior attracts defeat and aversion. He finds it impossible to delight in the joys of life. This definition fits abusers more than their victims who, on the contrary, seem optimistic and full of vitality.

However, numerous psychologists often consider the victims of abusive attacks as secret accomplices, establishing a pleasurable sadomasochistic relationship with their tormentor.

In sadomasochistic relationships of the erogenous type, both partners enjoy their mutual aggressiveness and hostility. *Who's Afraid of Virginia Woolf* by Edward Albee (1962) skillfully exemplifies this behavior. Within a framework of hidden symmetry, they keep the score even, knowing that if they want to, they can drop out of the game.

Abusive conduct, on the contrary, seeks to extinguish any trace of libido. Libido *is* life, so all signs of life, desire, and even reaction must be eroded to ultimately disappear completely.

In an abusive relationship, the balanced equation disappears, replaced by the dominance of one partner over the other and the impotence of the subjected partner to react and stop the struggle. This is primarily why we are dealing with real attacks on a person's identity. By previously establishing control the power to say no was taken away. Everything is dictated with no possibility for negotiation. The victim swept into an abusive situation tries to protect herself. When her masochistic traits, which exist in each one of us, are activated, she subsequently finds herself engulfed by a destructive relationship with no means of escape. She is "nailed" by her own inherent or reactive weakness. "Every individual wavers between a desire for independence and control, and a childish need to regain a condition of dependence, irresponsibility, and therefore, innocence."[3] The victim's basic mistake lies in not suspecting or fully appreciating the violence of the non-verbal messages. She reads the messages too literally, without translating what is actually said.

This allegedly masochistic propensity of victims to seek subjection is quickly picked up by abusers: "She likes it. She wants it." They know better than the victim what she feels: "I treat her that way because she loves it."

Masochism produces shame and guilt in contemporary society. One wants to seem aggressive and ready for anything. Not only do victims suffer as such, but they are ashamed of not being able to defend themselves.

The difference between victims of abusers and masochists is that the former, when they finally succeed with great effort in separating themselves, feel a sense of relief and tremendous liberation. They are not interested in suffering per se. They fall into the abuser's game during long periods because they are vital human beings and want to give, even the impossible task of giving life to an abuser: "With me, he'll change!"

This energy is accompanied by a certain fragility. Despite throwing themselves into the hopeless task of "resurrecting the dead," they feel uncertain of their own strength and become almost defiant in their course of action. They have to prove they are strong and capable because of their self-doubt and vulnerability. This makes them especially susceptible during the seduction phase, when the abuser validates them and increases their feeling of self-worth. Later on, their stubbornness becomes dangerous. They refuse to give up on the abuser because they cannot imagine that there's no solution and that change cannot be expected. As we shall see, they would feel guilty abandoning their partner.

If, as they say, masochism is a basic characteristic of the victim, why doesn't it manifest itself in other contexts, and why does it disappear after separation from the abuser?

THE VICTIM'S SCRUPLES°

Abusers generally attack their partners' weaknesses in a framework of guilt and lack of confidence. In order to destabilize and unsettle someone, fostering and encouraging feelings of blame and self-doubt is an obvious and effective procedure. In *The Trial* by Kafka,[4] Joseph K. is accused of having committed a crime, but he doesn't know what it consists of. He never stops trying to clear up the accusation to understand his blame. He doubts his own memory and ultimately convinces himself he's not himself.

The ideal victim is a conscientious person with a natural tendency to blame herself. In phenomenological psychiatry, this type of behavior is well known and described (for example, by Tellenbach[5]) as a predepressive personality of *typus melancolicus*. These people love order at work and in their relationships; they devote themselves to the people they most care about but hesitate to accept favors from others. The attachment to order and the desire to do good leads these people to assume more work than the average; this gives them a good conscience, but also makes them feel stretched to the limit with work and responsibilities.

The ethologist Boris Cyrulnik[6] correctly observed: "Melancholy individuals often marry unfeeling people. The less sensitive partner leads an emotionless little life serenely and calmly, the more so because the melancholy one, weighed down by permanent guilt, takes on all worries. He finds solutions to problems and manages their lives until the moment when, twenty years later, drained by endless sacrifice, he bursts into tears. He accuses his partner of skimming off the cream in their lives and leaving him the dregs."

Predepressives win the other's love by giving and putting themselves at his disposal; they also experience great satisfaction in being useful and giving pleasure. Narcissistic abusers take advantage of the situation. Victims can't tolerate misunderstandings and awkwardnesses, which they try to clear up. When difficulties pile up, they increase their efforts, feel overtaken by events, feel guilty, work harder and harder, get exhausted, become less efficient and, finally, in a vicious circle, feel more and more guilty. They'll go so far as to accuse themselves: "It's my fault if my partner is unhappy or abusive." If an error is committed, they'll assume the blame. This over-exaggerated conscience is linked to fear of failure which, together with remorse, causes them to suffer deeply and intensely.

They are equally vulnerable to other people's criticisms and judgments even when they aren't valid, and they continually justify themselves. Abusers, sensing this weakness, take delight in instilling doubt. "Maybe I was unconsciously guilty of what he's accusing me of?" Even if the accusations are unfair, they are no longer sure of their facts and ask themselves if they shouldn't assume the blame anyway.

Both the abuser and his victim behave in an extreme fashion. Their critical faculties become unbalanced, intensifying outwardly for the abuser and inwardly for the victim.

The victims virtually assume the other's guilt. They internalize the abusive element attacking them: the look, the gestures, and the words. The narcissistic abusers are able to project their guilt onto the victim. Denial is the only weapon an abuser needs to create doubt after an attack. In order to verify after the fact what has happened, certain victims resort to a variety of devices: they keep copies of mail, they arrange for a secret witness, or they tape telephone conversations.

The victims can generally manage to compensate for their underlying inferiority complex as long as they aren't made to feel guilty. This vulnerability toward feeling guilt is linked to a propensity to depression, but one that leads them to become hyperactive and strongly interactive with people instead of sad and lethargic.

Initially, the encounter with a narcissistic abuser can stimulate a victim to overcome gloomy melancholy. The English psychoanalyst Masud Khan describes how the passive nature of a predepressive woman makes her vulnerable to an abusive relationship: "It seems to me that the active will of the abuser is an illusion because the victim passively makes the demands and subscribes to that active will."[7] It starts as a game or intellectual joust. There is a challenge to meet: to be accepted or not as a partner by someone so demanding. The gloomy victims "stir up their emotions" and look for excitement in a relationship that will permit them to feel something and increase their sense of self-worth by opting for a difficult partner or situation.

One might say that potential victims have, on the one hand, a painful sensitivity linked to some childhood trauma and, on the other, great vitality. The abusers attack not the melancholy element but the vital one, where they can try to appropriate the vitality they perceive.

Because of their lack of narcissism, the victims are paralyzed by a rage that is repressed or internalized and prevents them from reacting.

THE VICTIM'S STRENGTH

Victims create envy because they can be too open about their feelings. They can't help describing their pleasure in such and such a possession and they don't know how not to show their happiness. In many societies, it's considered the "right thing" to disparage one's material or spiritual goods. Not conforming exposes one to envy.

In our society, which advocates equality, we tend to think that envy is, consciously or unconsciously, provoked by the envied person (for example, if one is robbed, one has too openly paraded one's wealth). The ideal victims of emotional abusers are those who, lacking confidence, feel obliged to exaggerate so they can present a better self-image at any cost.

It is therefore the victims' strong vitality that makes them "fair game" for the abuser.

They are compelled to give, and the abuser, to take: what an ideal encounter. Added to which, one refuses to take any blame while the other has a natural tendency to take it.

To make "the game worth the candle," victims must be up to the mark: they must know how to initially resist and, later, give in.

THE VICTIM'S NAIVETÉ

The victims appear naive and credulous. Incapable of imagining the fundamentally destructive nature of the other, they try to find logical explanations and avoid misunderstandings. "If I explain, he'll understand and apologize for his behavior." For anyone who's not abusive, it's impossible to imagine, from the very beginning, such a bottomless reservoir of ill-will and manipulation.

In order to deflect abusive maneuvers, victims try to be candid and justify themselves. When a sincere person opens up to a suspicious one, the latter usually gains the upper hand. The keys to their conduct that victims hand over to their aggressor only increase his contempt. Victims, when faced with an abusive attack, initially want to show understanding, adapt to the situation, and even forgive, because they love or admire the other person: "If he's that way, he must be unhappy. I'll reassure and heal him." In a wave of maternal feeling, they believe that they alone see what's happening and can help by giving them substance. They are like missionaries believing they can understand, justify, and forgive everything. Convinced that by talking it through they'll find a solution, they allow the abuser (who refuses to engage in any form of dialogue) to effectively checkmate them. Victims nourish the hope that the other will change and will finally understand and regret the pain he inflicts. They eternally hope that their explanations and justifications will solve misunderstandings and refuse to see that because one can intellectually and emotionally grasp a predicament is no reason to put up with it.

While emotional abusers remain frozen in their rigidity, the victims behave like chameleons: adapting, foreseeing what's expected of them by the abuser (consciously or unconsciously), and assuming more than their fair share of the blame. The manipulative methods work even better if the abuser has previously gained the victim's confidence (mother, father, spouse, or boss). The victims' forgiveness and lack of hard feelings makes them, strangely enough, powerful. It's intolerable and frustrating for the attacker to put up with what basically amounts to his victim's withdrawal: "I don't want to play the game." The victim becomes a living reproof, which only increases the attacker's hatred.

This vulnerability to being controlled often comes from childhood. We ask ourselves why the victims don't react. We observe their suffering and the surrender of their own lives and identity, yet they remain in the situation and even fear abandonment. We know that leaving would be their salvation but they are unable to act until they're disengaged from childhood traumas.

Alice Miller[8] has shown that an inhibited childhood, stifling the child for "his own good," crushes his will and leads him to repress his real feelings, his creativity, and his capacity to rebel. According to Miller, this predisposes a person to further subjection, either individual (emotional abuser) or collective (membership in a sect or totalitarian political party). With the ground laid since childhood, an individual will therefore be manipulated as an adult.

People who grew up in a repressive environment and were able to keep alive the possibility of reacting either verbally or in anger to humiliation and annoyances will be better equipped as adults to protect themselves against emotional abuse.

Victims use laser-like vision to detect the fragility and weaknesses of their abuser. Some also understand the pathological

nature of the behavior and shut themselves off when they detect
signs of falseness in their partner.

The victims become dangerous adversaries when they begin to articulate what they have intuitively understood. They must be silenced by terror.

PART III

CONSEQUENCES OF ABUSE

CHAPTER EIGHT

CONSEQUENCES OF THE "SEIZURE OF POWER" PHASE

Just as in a Hitchcock film, or in *The Spanish Prisoner* by David Mamet (1997), the plot follows the same outline: the victim doesn't see she's being manipulated; the mystery clears up with the help of outside intervention only when the violence becomes too obvious. The relationship begins in an atmosphere of charm and seduction and ends with terrifying psychopathic behavior. Abusers, however, leave clues that are only explained after the fact, when the victim has partially gotten out from under the control and understands the manipulative process.

We have just seen the victims paralyzed during the first phase; in the following phase, they will be destroyed.

WITHDRAWAL

Once control has been established and, unbeknownst to each other, the two "protagonists" withdraw in order to avoid conflict, the abuser advances subtly, with small, indirect strokes,

151

152 unsettling the other without provoking an open clash. The victim also withdraws and submits because she's afraid outright
discord would result in breaking up the relationship.

These avoidance tactics deflect the emergence of a violent
act without changing the conditions under which it could appear. The initial withdrawal maintains the relationship at the
cost of terrible damage to the victim. There exists an unspoken
alliance between the players. The victims of emotional abusers, in a delusional altruistic gesture, resign themselves to sub-
mitting to mistreatment. Even though they complain about
their partners' negative attitudes, they idealize certain other
aspects of their character (he is intelligent, a good parent,
etc.).

When the victim accepts submission, the relationship continues indefinitely on this basis: one of the partners becoming
more and more depressed, with her identity eroded, and the
other more and more dominant and assured of his power.

CONFUSION

Establishment of control makes the victims confused; they either don't dare or don't know how to complain. They act anesthetized, feel light-headed and unable to think. They describe
a real erosion and partial annihilation of their identity, along
with the deadening of what was alive and spontaneous inside
them. Although they sense they are unjustly treated, their confusion is such that they have no means of reacting. Unless one
also acts in a similarly abusive fashion, it is impossible when
confronted by an emotional abuser to have the last word. The
only possible answer is submission.

Confusion engenders stress. Physiologically, maximal stress
occurs when an individual is immobilized and living in conditions of great uncertainty. Victims often say that what creates

the most pain is not so much outright aggression as the uncertainty of whether they're partly to blame for the situation. When their abuser is unmasked, they say they are comforted.

"After everything he said to me, I ended up believing that maybe he was right and that I was crazy and hysterical. As he often had, he came to me one day with hatred in his eyes and said, in an icy tone of voice, that I was worthless and useless to anyone and I should just commit suicide. My neighbor was there by chance, and he hadn't seen her. She was terrified and encouraged me to file a complaint. This was an enormous relief to me. Someone had finally understood."

This highlights the importance of having unbiased witnesses present who haven't been influenced yet by either party. What makes a "seizure of power" so difficult to describe is the fact that it happens gradually: first, a stretching of the person's inner limits to their utmost, and then, the shattering of those limits. It makes pinpointing the exact onset of violence and abuse almost impossible.

In this psychological battle, the identity of the victims is profoundly eroded and their persona erased. They lose all self-esteem in both their own eyes and their abusers', who have only to get rid of them since they are now "hollow men."

DOUBT

When violence appears openly, still under the guise of control, it breaks upon a completely defenseless psyche that had been anesthetized by the control phase. What follows is almost unthinkable. Victims and eventual witnesses cannot believe what is unfolding before their eyes because, unless one is also an abuser, such violence without compassion is impossible. One ascribes feelings of guilt, sadness, or remorse to the abuser which he lacks completely. Incapable of understanding, the victim is shattered; she denies a reality she can't see. It can't have happened and it cannot be.

Subjected to this violent rejection, which is felt although verbally denied, the victims vainly try to understand and explain it to themselves. They look for the reasons this has happened and, not finding them, lose all confidence and become irritable or aggressive. They keep asking, "What have I done to be treated this way? There must be a reason." They need logic, but the process takes on an illogical life of its own and doesn't really have anything to do either with reality or with them. They often say to their aggressor, "Tell me what you reproach me for, tell me what I can do to improve our relationship," and he answers unyieldingly, "There's nothing to say, that's the way it is. You don't understand anything, anyway." Impotence and frustration are the worst outcomes.

Even if the victims acknowledge their share of responsibility for the violence, they also recognize that their presence alone would have triggered it. The abusers are always exonerated and the victims carry the blame. Disengagement from the relationship is now almost not an option because the first blows firmly nail in them a deeply unsettling guilt. Having once been found guilty, the victims assume responsibility for the relationship, although the presumed guilt bears no connection to reality. They internalize what threatens them.

People around them often reinforce the guilt because they, too, are confused and rarely know how to give support without passing judgment. They misinterpret wildly and make comments like, "You should be more this or that . . . Aren't you adding fuel to the fire? If he's that way, it must be because you've rubbed him the wrong way . . ."

Our society views guilt negatively: one shouldn't have spiritual downswings and one must always seem on top of things.

Since they say there's never smoke without fire, people tend to believe there's never guilt without blame. To an outsider, abusers saddle the victim with guilt.

STRESS

Tremendous inner tension is the high price paid for this submission: not allowing oneself to displease the other, soothing him when he's irritable, and forcing oneself not to react. This tension generates stress.

An organism reacts to stress by going into an alert state with the production of certain hormones, a lowering of the immune system, and a modification of neurological transmitters. Initially, this adaptation permits confrontation with the attack, whatever its origin. Everything gets back in order quickly when the stress stays on schedule and the individual succeeds in managing. But the activated neurological systems continue to function if the situation is prolonged or repeats itself at near intervals, overwhelming the subject's adaptive capacity. Persistent high levels of hormonal adaptation lead to symptoms that can become chronic.

The first symptoms of stress, depending on individual susceptibility, are palpitations, feelings of oppression, breathlessness, fatigue, insomnia, nervousness, irritability, headaches, digestive ailments, stomach pain, and psychological symptoms such as anxiety. Vulnerability to stress varies according to the individual. Experts for a long time thought it was genetic but now they have learned that this susceptibility can be gradually acquired when an individual is faced with chronic abuse.

Impulsive personalities are more sensitive to stress, while perverse abusers appear impervious to it. Their impulses are liberated by making others suffer. Perverse abusers are generally immune to combat neurosis after war's atrocities, as was the case in Vietnam.

Aggressors escape stress or internal pain by making the other responsible for all their problems. An escape route for victims is impossible because they don't comprehend the ongoing process. Nothing makes sense when contradictions abound and evidence is denied. They exhaust themselves trying to come up with answers which, inadequate, aggravate the violence, lead to pervasive wear and tear, and ultimately attack the neuroglandular function.

Since these pressures take place over long periods (months, sometimes years), the organism's resistance wears down and chronic anxiety appears. Functional and organic disorders can occur because of the aforementioned blows to the neurohormonal system.

After a series of failures, victims become discouraged and anticipate renewed disaster; this intensifies their stress and the hopelessness of attempts at defense.

Chronic stress can express itself by general anxiety, fear, or panic attacks that are difficult to control, and a permanent state of tension and hyper-alertness.

Emotional abusers, whether or not they achieve their goals, elicit in victims a violent element that they would prefer to ignore. At this stage in the process, all victims describe a state of fear. They are continually "on alert," watching for the partner's look, a stiffness in his gestures, or an icy tone covering up an unmanifested attack. They are afraid of the other's reaction, and his tenseness or coldness if they don't conform to expectations; they also expect wounding remarks, sarcasm, scorn, and contempt.

Terrified victims, whether they submit or react, are at fault whatever the circumstances. If they submit, abusers and perhaps those near to them will say they were decidedly born to be victims; otherwise, their "uptightness" will be highlighted and they will be blamed for the failure of the relationship as well as everything else, without regard for the truth.

They have a tendency, in order to avoid these attacks, to be nicer and nicer and more conciliatory. They operate under the illusion that the hatred will dissolve into love and kindness. They won't have that luck because the more generous one acts toward an abuser, the more the victim is destabilized. However, kindness and turning the other cheek in a sense increase one's superiority which, in turn, naturally reactivates the violence. If victims should happen to feel hatred in return, the abusers are delighted. This justifies them: "It's not I who hates him, but he who hates me."

ISOLATION

Confronting all this abuse, victims feel alone. How to talk to outsiders about what has happened and is happening? The subterranean damage and erosion are indescribable: what can you say about a look charged with hate, or a violence that shows up in unsaid allusions or implications? The violence is only obvious to the persecuted partner. How could friends possibly imagine what goes on? Even if they wanted to know the reality of the abuse, they would be troubled and horrified. Generally, even those closest to the situation keep their distance: "We don't want to get mixed up in *that*!"

Victims doubt their own intuition and think they must be exaggerating. When attacks occur in front of witnesses, the victims, ever protective of the abuser, judge their reactions excessive; they are then faced with the paradox of defending their abuser.

CHAPTER NINE

Long-Term Consequences

SHOCK

Shock occurs when the victims become conscious of their abuse. Until that point, they had probably been more confident than suspicious. They would have refused to recognize their subjection or their overly tolerant attitude toward an obvious lack of respect, even if it had been remarked upon by outsiders. They suddenly realize they have been manipulated.

They are wounded and at a loss as to how to proceed. Their world collapses. The far-reaching consequences of the trauma result from their unpreparedness and surprise because they had been paralyzed by the other's control. Hurt and anguish blend together, after the emotional shock. Some victims describe it as an actual physical attack or a violent emotional intrusion evoking impotence and overwhelming despair: "It's like a stab to the chest. I feel like a boxer who's down and continues to be pummeled!"

Amazingly, one rarely sees angry or rebellious behavior, even after victims have made the decision to separate. Even though the victims can acknowledge the injustice of what they've been through, they still can't rebel or liberate themselves by means of anger. Anger comes later and even then, because it is censored, will be ineffectual. Victims must be completely outside the control framework in order to really experience liberating anger.

Once they become aware of the manipulation, victims feel swindled. The same refrain of having been cheated, abused, and not respected constantly recurs. Too late, they discover they are victims who have been toyed with and forced to lose their self-esteem and sense of dignity. They are ashamed of their reactions to the manipulation: "I should have reacted sooner!" "Why didn't I see anything?" They are suddenly conscious that their quasi-pathological compliance permitted the abuser's violence.

These people sometimes thirst for revenge but more often they seek rehabilitation and an acknowledgment of their identity. They hope for apologies, which will not be forthcoming, from their abuser. If amends are made, they come much later from witnesses or passive accomplices who were also manipulated and joined in the abusive attacks.

DECOMPENSATION*

The victims, weakened after the control phase, now feel directly attacked. An individual's capacity to resist is not unlimited; it progressively erodes and leads to psychological exhaustion. After a certain amount of stress, adaptive techniques no longer work. Decompensation takes place, and long-term ailments may also occur.

Psychiatrists generally encounter victims at the decompensation stage. They suffer from pervasive anxiety, depression, or

*Decompensation: Deterioration or failure of regulating mechanisms, including psychological defenses.

psychosomatic illnesses. Decompensation can lead to violence in more impulsive patients. Abusers often take this as justification for their behavior.

At this stage, when we suggest to victims of emotional abuse in organizations that they take a leave, surprisingly, they rarely accept. "If I stop, it'll only be worse. They'll make me pay!" Fear accepts everything.

Depression is linked to exhaustion and too much stress. Victims feel empty, tired, and without energy. Nothing interests them. They can't think about or concentrate even on the most mundane subjects. They will sometimes contemplate suicide. The risk of suicide becomes greater during the period when they suddenly realize they've been cheated and their damages will never be compensated.

In cases of suicide or attempted suicide, abusers are bolstered in their belief that the other was weak, disturbed, or crazy, and therefore their conduct was not wicked. After abusive attacks, the aggressor manages to seem all-powerful, showing his high moral standards and wisdom. Disillusionment for the trusting victim is crushing. Events likely to trigger a state of depression are not just experiences of mourning or separation, but also include the loss of an ideal. More than a difficult or dangerous situation, the latter engenders feelings of uselessness, powerlessness, or defeat. A sense of humiliation or of having been trapped can cause depression.

In a situation of abuse or harassment, after failure to establish any kind of dialogue, a permanent anxiety settles over the victim like a cloud, and is fed by continual attacks. This chronic state of apprehension and anticipation often needs to be medically regulated.

In other victims, the response can be psychosomatic: ulcers, cardiovascular illness, rashes, etc. Some lose weight and become weak. The attacks on their spirit that they had seemed unaware of but were destroying their identity need to be physically expressed.

Psychosomatic ailments are not a direct result of abuse but, rather, stem from the subject's inability to react. No matter what he does, he is wrong, and no matter what he does, he is guilty.

A direct result of abusive provocation for still others is behavioral in nature. Hysterics in public or attacks on the abuser are vain attempts to be heard, which instead will be turned against the victim: "I warned you, he is completely ill!"

Impulsive as well as predatory abuse can lead to violent crime, although it's more likely in the former. Emotional abusers, in order to prove the victims are bad, will go so far as to arouse violent reactions in them. In the movie *Passage à l'Acte* (1996) by Francis Girod, a perverse abuser makes his psychiatrist kill him. He has played the game out to its fullest extent. Sometimes the victim turns the violence against himself and commits suicide because it is the only way to get rid of his aggressor.

Another little-known consequence of traumatism is dissociation (Spiegel, 1993[1]), which can be described as a shattering of personality. It is defined in *DSM-IV*[2] as a disorder affecting normally integrated functions such as conscience, memory, identity, or perception of the environment. It's a defense mechanism against the fear, pain, or impotence brought on by an event so alien to the normal condition that the psyche has no recourse but to distort it or chase it from consciousness.

Dissociation separates the bearable from the unbearable, which is driven from memory. It filters experience, thereby easing pain and providing some protection to the soul.

The phenomenon of dissociation reinforces control, and this added difficulty must be taken into consideration during therapy.

SEPARATION

Victims can react in two different ways as the danger threatening them becomes clearer:

1. Submit and accept domination, allowing the abuser to freely continue toward his goal of destructive annihilation.
2. Rebel and fight, in order to leave.

Certain individuals who have been controlled too long or too intensely are incapable of flight or war. They will sometimes consult a therapist or psychiatrist, but announce right away that they won't make any fundamental changes in the situation. They would just like to "hang on" in their current situation, putting "a good face on it" without too many symptoms. They generally prefer a drug-related treatment to extended psychotherapy. When depression persists and when the prescribed drugs become ineffective, the psychiatrist may reintroduce the idea of therapy. Once abuse has taken root, however, the victim's departure is the only solution.

Victims react most often when they see the violent tactics used on another person or when they are able to find an ally or some form of outside support.

Separation, when it occurs, is accomplished by the victims and never the abusers. Victims separate with emotions of pain and guilt because the narcissistic abusers themselves pose as abandoned victims and find new pretexts for violence. During the separation process, abusers always consider themselves the wronged party and become litigious, taking advantage of the fact that the victim, hurrying to end the ordeal, is still ready to make concessions. In a couple, blackmail and pressure are exerted in two areas: children, where applicable, and financial settlements. It's not unusual for victims to be sued in an organizational framework, because they are always considered guilty. Either way, the abuser claims injury, whereas the victim is the one who loses everything.

EVOLUTION

Even if the victims, during the separation, lose all contact with their abuser, it is impossible to deny the dramatic consequences of a period in their lives when they were basically reduced to the position of object. Every memory or new event will take on a different meaning as it relates to that time and experience.

Liberation comes to the victims in a wave of euphoria, when they distance themselves physically from the abuser: "I can finally breathe!" After the initial shock, interest in work and leisure activities and curiosity about the world and people, in fact, everything that had been blocked by dependence, reappears. However, the new way is not without difficult passages.

Some victims of emotional abuse come through with no serious psychological after-effects other than horrible memories that seem under control. This is especially true when the abuse has been short-lived and took place outside the family. They accept the disagreeable aspects of a traumatic situation they have experienced.

Attempts to forget more often lead to the appearance of delayed psychological or somatic problems, as if the suffering had become a foreign body, both active and inaccessible, in the soul.

Past abusive violence can leave mild traces, compatible with leading an almost normal life. The victims appear psychologically undamaged although vague symptoms persist; these symptoms are like attempts to belie what was actually experienced. They may include general anxiety, chronic fatigue, or insomnia, headaches, and psychosomatic ailments (eczema, ulcers, etc.); dependent behavior is particularly prevalent (bulimia, alcoholism, drug use). When these victims consult their internist, they are prescribed a tranquilizer because since the victim doesn't talk about it, the connection isn't made between past experience and present ailments.

Occasionally, victims complain of feeling uncontrollable aggression after the fact; this can stem from the impossibility of defending themselves during the abuse period or it may be interpreted as transferred violence. Other victims will exhibit a series of symptoms related to post-traumatic stress. This corresponds to the definition of traumatic neurosis developed after World War I[3] and studied further on veterans of the Vietnam War. The diagnosis was later used to describe the psychological consequences of natural disasters, armed assault, and rape. Only very recently has it been used in connection with conjugal violence.[4]

One normally doesn't relate post-traumatic stress to victims of emotional abuse because it is reserved for people who have had their (or someone else's) physical safety threatened. However, L. Croq, a French victimology specialist, considers individuals who have been menaced, abused, or defamed as psychological victims.[5] These victims, like war victims, have been in a virtual "state of siege" condition that obliged them to be permanently on the defensive.

Abuse and humiliation are etched in memory and relived repeatedly through images and thoughts, sometimes provoking intense feelings of dread that an identical situation might imminently recur; at night these feelings and thoughts cause insomnia or nightmares. Victims need to talk about traumatic events but evoking the past produces the same psychosomatic symptoms as fear: memory and concentration lapses, bulimia or loss of appetite, and increased alcohol and tobacco consumption.

Over the long term, fear of confronting the abuser and the memory of a traumatic situation result in tactics to avoid thinking about the stressful event or anything that evokes the pain connected to it. This distancing to try and escape memories reduces interest in previously important activities and restricts emotional scope. At the same time, trouble sleeping or hyper-alertness continues.

Almost all victims of emotional abuse describe reliving a painful past, but some manage to disengage themselves by getting involved in outside activities, be it professional or charitable.

In time, although the experience is not forgotten, it becomes less intrinsically a part of one's psyche. Victims say that ten or twenty years later, they still feel distressed when they see images of their abuser. Even if they now lead full and satisfying lives, memories like this bring sharp pain. Any trace of abuse in a relationship will make them run as fast as they can because the trauma has developed extra-sensitive antennae in them. The important long-term consequences of abuse victims in an organizational structure are often only perceived when, after a long absence from the job, it is suggested they return to work. This retriggers the symptoms—anguish, insomnia, dire thoughts—and the patient enters a vicious circle of relapse: leave from work, back to work, relapse, etc., which can result in permanent rejection.

If victims are unable to throw off the shackles of control, their life stops at the moment of trauma: their vitality is dulled, their joy in life deadens, and their personal initiative disappears. They complain of being wronged and battered and they

become sour and irritable, retreating to an anti-social existence filled with bitter recriminations. These victims endlessly
repeat their sad stories, which those around them find hard to
take: "It's ancient history, you should think about something
else!" Victims in general, from families or organizations, rarely
demand vengeance. They do want acknowledgment of what
they have undergone in spite of the fact that it is impossible to
make up for injustice. In business, financial reparation hardly
compensates for the suffering endured. It's useless to expect
remorse or regret from an emotional abuser: the suffering
of others is not important. Repentance will only come from
those who were silent witnesses and accomplices: only they can
express their regrets and give the abused person back his or
her dignity.

CHAPTER TEN

PRACTICAL ADVICE FOR THE COUPLE AND THE FAMILY

O ne never wins against an abuser. But one can learn something about oneself.

The temptation is great for victims, in order to defend themselves, to resort to the same devices as their aggressors. Nevertheless, as victim, one is less perverse, and it is difficult to see how the situation could be reversed. One is strongly advised against using the same tactics; basically, legal intervention is the only recourse.

REORIENTATION

It is important for the victim to first recognize the abusive process, which consists in making her responsible for the conflict in the conjugal or family framework, and subsequently, to analyze the problem objectively, putting aside the question of guilt. She must abandon the ideal of absolute tolerance and acknowledge that someone she loves or has loved manifests elements in his character that are dangerous for her and that she must protect herself against.

167

In another area, parents must also learn to detect individuals who are directly or indirectly harmful to their children, which is not easy when the person may be a near relative.

One remains defenseless until one is out from under the control of the other and can accept the fact that the abuser, despite the feelings one still has or has had, is dangerous and evil.

When the victim stops playing the game, it unleashes a burst of violence in the abuser that will lead him to go too far. One may, at this point, rely on the abuser's methods to beat him at his own game without actually using them; that is a trap to avoid at all costs. Because the abuser's ultimate goal is to contaminate the other and to make her become a "bad" person, the only viable victory lies in *not* becoming like him and acting abusive. To accomplish this, recognizing his tactics and behavioral mode is paramount in defusing his abuse.

An essential rule when one is tormented by an emotional abuser is to stop justifying oneself. It's an insidious temptation because an abuser's words are stuffed with lies uttered in the greatest bad faith. Any explanation or justification can only entrap the victim deeper. Any vagueness or mistake on her part, even when well meant, can be used against her. Once a victim is in an abuser's line of fire, all kinds of utterances will be used as ammunition. Silence becomes golden.

To an abuser, the victim is wrong, or at least, everything she says or does is suspect. Her intentions are malicious and her words can only be lies. Abusers cannot imagine anyone not lying.

The preceding stages in the process have allowed the victim to see that dialogue and explanations are worthless. In case of direct contact, it's important to give oneself time to think of the proper response, but generally, the presence of a third party is the best solution.

After a separation, if the abuse persists by telephone, one can change the number or just leave the answering machine on. Mail should probably be opened by someone else, because abusive letters reintroduce small touches of poison and suffering, unsettling the victim anew.

ACTION

Because the victim has until now, because of the control factor, been overly conciliatory, she must now change her strategy and act firmly without fear of conflict. Her determination will oblige the abuser to show his hand. Any change of attitude in the victim will generally provoke, at this time, a stream of abuse and provocation. The abuser wants to increase her sense of blame: "You definitely have no compassion." "One can never talk to you."

No longer paralyzed, she can break open the vicious circle. By throwing the crisis out into the open, she may seem the aggressor, but she must make this choice because it's the only way for change to occur. The crisis acts like an earthquake tremor, giving the victim a means of escape from the control vise and a chance for life to begin again. It's the only way to work out a compromise or possible solution to the situation. The longer the crisis is delayed, the more violent it will be when it finally arrives.

PSYCHOLOGICAL RESISTANCE

In order to resist psychologically, support is essential. Sometimes an expression of confidence from one person, in whatever context, enables the victim to regain hers. However, one can't always trust the advice from the immediate circle of family and friends or anyone wanting to mediate, because neutrality is impossible for those closest to the situation. They themselves are generally disoriented and drawn to one side or the other. Emotional abuse allows one to quickly sort out trustworthy friendships. Some people who seem close to the victim allow themselves to be manipulated, become suspicious, or reproach the victim. Others, not understanding the situation, choose to run for cover. Really valuable support comes from those who know it's important just to be there, available and non-judgmental; those individuals who, no matter what happens, will remain true to themselves.

LEGAL INTERVENTION

In some cases, legal intervention is the only solution. Using this objectively allows one to see things in their true light and enables one to say no.

Often a judgment can only be rendered with evidence as backup. A battered woman can show her bruises; when she defends herself, that defense is legitimate. A humiliated and wounded woman, with no clear-cut proof to present, has difficulty making herself heard. When a person decides to separate from her emotional abuser, she should try to find a way for the abuse to take place in front of a third party who will testify. She must also keep any written evidence. Alienation of affection, if proved, can be grounds for divorce.

In the case of unmarried individuals, the problem becomes more complicated. It is only after the aggression has been classified as a misdemeanor that justice can intervene.

Victims hesitate to sue when they, too, may have reacted violently. However, provocation precludes a legal penalty. The legal system then acknowledges that the victim's violent actions were justified by the partner's insults.

Judges can be wary when dealing with abusive manipula- 171
tion. They fear being manipulated themselves and, seeking
conciliation at any price, protect themselves on both sides by
taking weak measures too late. The same insidious and under-
mining invalidation process develops with the involuntary and
ignorant complicity of the mediator. Seeking to obtain a real
dialogue with an abuser is illusory because he will always be
too clever and will use the mediating process to further disqualify his partner. Conciliation must not happen to the detriment of one of the parties. The victim has already greatly
suffered and cannot be asked to make further concessions.

The only way to protect the victims and prevent them from
reacting to direct or indirect provocation is to put in place strict
legal measures and to avoid any contact between the parties,
hoping that someday the abuser will find another victim and
let this one go.

When there are children involved, particularly if they too
are being manipulated, the victim must save herself so she can
then protect them from the abusive relationship. She must
override reluctance on the children's part, who would prefer
that nothing change. The legal system must take protective
measures in order to avoid any contact capable of reactivating
the abusive relationship.

CHAPTER ELEVEN

PRACTICAL ADVICE
FOR THE
WORKPLACE

REORIENTATION

It is very important to recognize the process of emotional abuse and, whenever possible, to analyze it. If one feels one's dignity or psychological integrity damaged because of the ongoing hostility of one or more people over a long period of time, it is most probably a matter of emotional abuse.

Ideally, one should react as soon as possible so as not to become mired in a situation where the only solution can be departure.

At the first recognizable sign of emotional abuse, it is vital to take note of any form of provocation or aggression. Just as in the case of emotional abuse in families, the difficulty in defending oneself lies in a lack of clear proof.

The victim must therefore collect all traces and indications of abuse, write down a description of the offenses committed, and photocopy any evidence that might shore up the defense.

It would also be helpful to secure the participation of witnesses. Unfortunately, in a context of emotional abuse, colleagues will often disassociate themselves from the victim out of fear of reprisal; in addition, when an abuser targets his prey, people generally prefer to sit tight and not say anything. Nevertheless, a single witness is often enough to give credence to a victim's allegations.

FINDING HELP WITHIN THE ORGANIZATION

In order to battle early and effectively, one must first look for help within the organization. Too often, employees only react when trouble has already begun and an intent to fire has been decided on. Finding help can be difficult when the situation has deteriorated to this point. It means the executive in charge, if not the instigator of the process, has been unable to deal effectively with the problem. When moral support is unavailable within one's immediate environment, help must be sought elsewhere in the organization.

The employee can evade the process of emotional abuse at each preliminary stage if he can find someone who knows how to listen, but once abuse has been firmly established, escape becomes more problematic.

If the company is sufficiently big, one must first seek help at the department of human resources. Unfortunately, the heads of these departments are often better trained to deal with administrative and legal matters than communication problems between employees. People are asked to produce results in organizations, and that includes those in the human resources department. Problems of emotional abuse are unquantifiable and difficult to concretize, so they are often avoided and shelved.

If the human resources person has been unwilling or unable to help, one should approach the company doctor or psychologist. He can, as a first step, assist the victim in articulating the problem; later, he can make others within the organization aware of the serious consequences of emotional abuse. His role as a mediator is only possible if he has the confidence and trust of the organization's executives and, in addition, knows the people involved very well. In most cases, the doctor is contacted too late in the process to do more than suggest a medical leave of absence or work stoppage. The doctor's position is a sensitive one because his evaluation can be of serious consequence to the employee. Many victims feel that because he, too, is a salaried employee, they can't be entirely sure of his independence from the organization that is directly or indirectly abusing them.

PSYCHOLOGICAL RESISTANCE

One must be in good psychological health in order to defend oneself without being at a disadvantage. We have seen that the first stage of emotional abuse consists in destabilizing the victim. He must therefore consult a psychiatrist or psychologist to ensure that he has the strength to defend himself. To diminish stress and its damaging effects on health, the only solution may be to stop work. Many victims initially refuse to do this because they are afraid it will only aggravate the conflict. If the person is depressed, an anti-depressant is essential. The person can only resume work when he is completely ready to fight back in self-defense. This can result in a relatively long absence from work (sometimes several months), which will eventually become a long sick leave. Psychiatrists and Social Security medical advisers will undertake to protect the victim and work toward solving the professional questions raised; theoretically the solutions should be formulated within a legal framework.

A victim cracks. A leave of absence for depression prescribed by her doctor is just what the abuser and the management of the organization have wanted. When the victim announces that her sick leave is ending, management suggests she prolong it. The doctor refuses, arguing that because the problem was work-related, it should be settled between the employee and the organization. The victim returns to work and is blamed for not having taken care of herself.

Another victim, harassed and abused for several months by her boss, is given a leave of absence. She relapses every time she returns to work. The boss becomes so threatening that the victim sues. To avoid censure by the arbitration board, the boss agrees to lay off the employee, but he drags his feet in doing the necessary paperwork. The victim, still on a leave of absence, improves. Should she resume work while waiting for her dismissal to become effective? The medical advisor has decided that she should not. He prefers to protect the victim by prolonging her leave of absence until dismissal.

Given that the abuser's game consists in provoking and putting the victim in the wrong by arousing her anger and making her confused, the victim must learn to resist. In this kind of situation, it's sometimes easier to submit than to resist and risk conflict. No matter what their feelings might be, I advise victims to try to appear indifferent, to smile and reply with humor and without sarcasm. They must remain imperturbable and avoid playing the abuser's game. They must let the abuser have his say and stay calm and cool, meanwhile, taking note of every abusive act in order to prepare for defense.

To protect her professional reputation, the victim must be irreproachable. The searchlight is on her, even if her abuser is not an immediate superior. She is watched and observed so that management can understand the situation. The slightest error or lack of punctuality will be held as proof of her responsibility in the abusive process.

She must also learn to practice distrust by locking her desk drawers and taking with her, even if it's just out to lunch, her agenda and any files she might be working on. Naturally, victims are reluctant to act this way. It is only when the situation becomes a full-blown crisis that they will prepare a defense file for the arbitration board.

To regain their sense of judgment and independent thought, the victims should begin filtering communication differently, which will allow them to readjust to reality by deciphering messages literally and precisely and by refusing to decode innuendoes and implications.

This pattern of conduct presumes that the victim will be able to keep her cool. She must learn not to react to her abuser's provocation, which can be difficult for someone who may have been targeted because of her impulsiveness. The victim has to relinquish her usual patterns of behavior and practice serenity and calm while awaiting her turn. It is important that she believe deeply that she is in the right and that, sooner or later, her problem will be heard.

ACTION

Contrary to my advice in family abuse cases, where one must stop justifying oneself in order to throw off the abuser's control, in a professional framework, one must rigorously counterattack abusive communication. One can anticipate abuse by eliminating any ambiguity present in orders and directives and precisely clarifying any uncertainties. If doubts persist, the employee should request explanations in a formal interview. In case of a refusal, he must put his request in writing. This can serve as evidence of a lack of dialogue between the partners, should conflict later arise. It is preferable to be considered abnormally mistrustful, even paranoid, than to be found in error. It is not a bad thing for the abuser to feel uneasy at this reversal and to know that the victim will resist future abusive tactics.

Sometimes when the victim believes there's no solution to the situation in the offing or fears dismissal, he will turn to either his union or a personnel representative. When the union becomes involved, it launches an open battle and must negotiate a settlement prior to the victim's departure from the job. Mediation at this level can be hard to obtain because personnel representatives are more used to settling claims than listening and mediating a case of emotional abuse and harassment.

The law allows an employee to be accompanied by a person of his choice in a preliminary arbitration interview. This might be a labor union delegate or a personnel adviser from an outside union who will defend employees from other small organizations.

In abuse cases, it is important for the victim to have complete confidence in the ombudsperson and to know that he or she won't be manipulated.

Simple resignation would represent too easy a victory for the abuser. If the victim has to leave—and at this point resignation is his safeguard—he must fight to ensure that his departure is correctly handled.

In cases where no valid professional reason for dismissal exists, the employer can cite incompatibility. This motive is seldom used because it must be sustained by hard facts or it will be thrown out by the arbitration board, especially in the case of long-time employees. An exception might be made in a case where there are numerous concrete allegations involving large numbers of people.

If the employer has not stopped the abusive process, it is unlikely management will initiate a settlement; therefore, the responsibility lies with the employee.

LEGAL INTERVENTION

EMOTIONAL ABUSE

Currently there is no law banning emotional abuse, so it is difficult to take one's employer to court, which in any case is a long and painful process.

Nonetheless, a resolution adopted by the General Assembly of the United Nations as an amendment to the fundamental principles of justice, relating to victims of crime and abuse of power, defines victims of the latter as follows: "By victims we mean people who, individually or collectively, have suffered prejudice, most particularly, injury to their physical or mental well-being, moral suffering, material loss, or grave injury to their fundamental rights from acts or omissions which do not yet constitute a violation of national penal law, but which represent violations of acknowledged international standards relating to the rights of man."

The French work code does not protect victims of emotional abuse. One only finds the vague term "misconduct" as an addendum to articles of law concerning the disciplinary power of an employer: "In principle, the type of conduct targeted here does not justify dismissal where it concerns the employee's private life. This would not be the case, however, if the accusations are capable of creating problems within the organization. Repeated acts of indecency from an employee toward his female colleagues would justify dismissal for serious cause."

In Sweden, emotional abuse in an organization has been an offense since 1993. It is also recognized in Germany, Italy, and Australia. In the United States, a proposed law which has been adopted by a number of states, including New York, states that "one who by extreme and outrageous conduct intentionally or recklessly causes severe emotional distress to another is subject to liability for such emotional distress, and if bodily harm to the other results from it, for such bodily harm."[1] In Switzerland, in the framework of private enterprise, the federal law on work concerning hygienic measures and the protection of health, as well as Article 328 of the code concerning obligations dealing with the protection of health and an employee's individuality, apply: "The employer must take any measures necessary to assure and improve the protection of health and to guarantee the physical and psychological health of his employees. . . . The fight against abuse endangers the physical and psychological health of the abused person."

However, when the abuser is an employer who systematically uses abusive procedures to terrorize a member of his workforce, he must be legally stopped, particularly if the circumstances involve physical or sexual violence. Abusers who are reluctant to confront an employee directly will certainly avoid dealing within a legal framework. They are afraid and, therefore, will negotiate the terms of a dismissal. Abusers, in effect, dread trials that might publicly reveal their terrible conduct. They first use intimidation to silence their victims, and if that doesn't work, they lean toward negotiation, posing as victims of a crafty and mentally twisted employee.

Moral abuse has such power to do harm that it is difficult to contain. If individuals and organizations don't find ways to instill civility and respect for other human beings, it will become necessary to legislate emotional abuse based on the model of sexual abuse.

To my knowledge, there is currently no organization dedicated to specifically advising and helping victims of emotional abuse.

SEXUAL ABUSE

Since 1992, sexual abuse has been a criminal offense and a violation of the work code in France. The law forbids an employee to be reprimanded or dismissed for having submitted to or refused acts of sexual abuse.

Article 21 of the work code concerning sexual abuse only deals with harassment as abuse of power: "No employee may be penalized or dismissed for having submitted to or refused acts of abuse from their employer, his representative, or any other person who, abusing the authority conferred on him by his office, gave orders, pronounced threats, imposed constraints, or exerted pressure of any kind on this employee in the expectation of obtaining favors of a sexual nature for himself or a third party."

We see that the law only forbids one kind of sexual abuse (blackmail), but this kind of violence should be forbidden in and of itself without regard to bureaucratic considerations or threats of dismissal.

In France, initiating proceedings is an uphill battle because victims come up against all kinds of resistance and impediments. Abuse, even sexual and even with proof, is not seriously taken into account. Just as when dealing with sexual attacks, resistance can range from police refusal to register a complaint to the disqualification of facts by judges. These files are often labeled "discontinued" or "not to be reopened."

Sexual abuse is a worldwide problem. In Japan, sexual abuse complaints multiply proportionately since it is customary, even for women executives, to invite important clients to bars, first-class restaurants, or "no-pant clubs" (bars where the waitresses wear nothing under their mini-skirts). In France, the new law on equality of the sexes in the workplace, enacted in April 1999, provides resolutions against the practice. Instead of mocking Americans for their over-zealousness in suing over sexual abuse, we would do better to establish preventive policies ourselves and impose respect for the individual in the workplace.

ORGANIZING PREVENTION

Abuse is established when dialogue stops and the abused person cannot make himself heard. Prevention therefore means reintroducing dialogue and real communication. In this context, the organization's medical expert plays an important role. He can, at the request of management, initiate inclusive meetings to find solutions to the problem. In organizations with more than fifty employees, committees on working conditions, hygiene, and security exist or can be formed. In this framework, management, personnel delegates, and medical advisers can work together toward intervention. Unfortunately, these collaborative examples are usually instigated only in cases of physical risk or with respect to work norms.

Prevention should also include educating those in responsible positions to really focus on the human beings in question and not just on their productivity. In more specialized groups backed by psychiatrists or psychologists trained in victimology, people could learn to "meta-communicate," that is, communicate about communication in order to know how to intervene before the process of abuse gets going. This is accomplished by identifying what it is in the other person that irritates the abuser and, conversely, by making him really "hear" the victim's strongly expressed feelings. Once the process of abuse is set in place, it's too late. Union management knows how to negotiate indemnity in dismissal cases, but they are less comfortable understanding human relationships. Why not educate them and give them the necessary tools to intervene in dysfunctional or organizational situations before they reach the dismissal stage?

One would hope that protective clauses against emotional abuse be a part of both private and public organizational policy and that strict legal standards be adopted by the workplace.

Prevention means, above all, information for victims, employees, and organizations. It is important to recognize that emotional abuse exists, that it is fairly common, and that it can be avoided. The media can also play an important role in disseminating this information.

Only human beings can correct human situations. Abusive situations develop because they're either encouraged or tolerated. It is up to executive management and boards of directors to reintroduce the concept of respect for others within their sphere.

CHAPTER TWELVE

TAKING CHARGE
PSYCHOLOGICALLY

THE HEALING PROCESS

As we have seen, emotional abuse settles in so insidiously that it is often difficult to recognize and, in turn, to defend oneself against. Taking charge can rarely be accomplished alone. When one is confronted by a clearly aggressive attack, psychotherapeutic help is often necessary. One can say that a psychological attack has taken place when the dignity of an individual has been harmed by the conduct of another individual. The victims' mistake lies in not demanding respect and in not realizing soon enough that the limits and boundaries of their integrity have been crossed. Instead, they absorbed the assaults on their identity like sponges. They must define what is acceptable to them and, in so doing, define themselves.

THE CHOICE OF PSYCHOTHERAPY

The first act enabling a victim to become proactive lies in the choice of psychotherapy. In order to ensure against falling back into a manipulative framework, the victim must check out the

183

therapist's background. When in doubt, it is probably preferable to choose a psychiatrist or psychologist because in today's
world, all sorts of seductive new therapies have proliferated,
promising quick healing but functioning more like cults. No serious therapeutic system can avoid turning the patient back on
him- or herself. The easiest solution might be for the victim to
ask for a recommendation, either from a trusted friend or from
a private physician. The victim mustn't hesitate to interview
several therapists to ultimately select the one he or she trusts
the most and feels the most comfortable with. Feelings are the
springboard from which the patient will judge the therapist's
ability to help.

Benevolent neutrality, which can seem like coldness in some
therapists, is not advised for the patient whose ego has been
wounded. The psychoanalyst Ferenczi, for some time a disci-
ple and friend of Freud's, broke with him over the subject of
trauma and analytic technique. In 1932, he wrote: "In analysis,
that cold reserve and antipathy and professional hypocrisy toward the patient which he feels in every limb isn't all that
different from the former state of things, which in childhood
used to make him sick."[1] The psychotherapist's silence echoes
the abuser's refusal to communicate and leads to secondary
victimization.

Taking on victims of abuse should make us question the
effectiveness of our knowledge and therapeutic techniques by
aligning ourselves with the victim without simultaneously
setting ourselves up as all-powerful. We must learn to think
unconventionally and without certainties and dare to doubt
Freudian dogma. Most psychoanalysts who take on these victims no longer religiously follow Freud when it comes to the
reality of trauma: "Analytical technique applied to victims
should be redefined both in terms of psychological and event-
related reality. The primacy accorded inner conflict to the det-

riment of objective reality explains the fact that psychoanalysts
undervalue the research on trauma and its psychological impact."[2]

Psychotherapists should show flexibility and find a new and
more active, kind, and stimulating way to treat patients. As
long as the patient has not escaped from under the abuser's
control, a typical psychoanalytical cure with all its attendant
frustration will not help. The victim will only relapse into a
different form of control.

LABELING ABUSE

It is important that the therapist accept as a given the trauma
originating from outside abuse. Patients often have difficulty
remembering the past relationship, on the one hand, because
what they want is to flee into forgetting and, on the other,
because what they might or could say is still unthinkable for
them. They will need time and the support of psychotherapy
to gradually be able to articulate it. The disbelief of the therapist would constitute a supplementary violence, and his silence
would make him the abuser's accomplice. Certain patients
who have experienced abusive situations say that when they've
tried to talk about it to a therapist, the therapist didn't want to
hear what they had to say and indicated he was more interested
in the intrapsychological aspect of the case than the violence as
it was actually lived.

Naming abusive manipulation doesn't lead the person to relive the situation; on the contrary, it frees him from denial and
guilt. To gain freedom is to lift the weight of ambiguity from
words and from what is left unspoken. The therapist, whatever
theories he espouses, must feel sufficiently free in his practice to
communicate this freedom to his patient and help him get out
from under the emotional control.

It is impossible to treat the victim of an abuser (emotional or sexual) without putting everything in context. The therapist should initially help his patient throw light on the abusive process and avoid giving this process a neurotic connotation; the patient should describe it and then assess herself and her vulnerability and evaluate what actually constitutes outside abuse. In addition to a recognition of the abusive nature of the relationship, there should be an awareness of how the hold over the victim was initially established. By receiving the tools to recognize abusive strategies, the victim will no longer allow herself to be seduced or to take pity on her abuser.

One must also ask the patient to express the anger she couldn't feel while under the abuser's control and be able to say and feel previously censored emotions; if the patient can't find the words, she must be helped to verbalize her feelings.

LEAVING

When embarking on therapeutic treatment in the context of abuse, the victim should not ask initially, "How did I get myself into this situation?" but instead, "How can I leave immediately?"

In its early stages, the therapy should be comforting and allow the victim to shed her fear and guilt. The patient must clearly feel that the therapist is there for her and sympathizes with her suffering. Reinforcing the victim's psyche and fusing together its intact elements gives the victim sufficient confidence to dare to refuse something that might be deadly for her. This goal can only be reached when the victim has gained sufficient maturity to confront her abuser and say no.

Once the abuse has been acknowledged, the victim should rethink the events of the past in relation to what she has learned about that abuse. Her reading of what was happening had been wrong. She had registered hundreds of facts that didn't make sense as they occurred because they were all disassociated; now, in a kind of perverse logic, they become clear. She courageously must ask herself what meaning such and such a word or situation had. Very often, victims had the feeling that what was being said and done to them was harmful, but unable to imagine any criteria other than their own values, they submitted.

FREEDOM FROM GUILT

Therapy must not under any circumstances reinforce the victim's guilt by making her seem responsible for her position as victim. Although she is not responsible, she will continue to blame herself for the situation. As long as she remains under the abuser's control, she will be riddled with doubt and guilt— "How am I responsible for this abuse?"—and this guilt will prevent her from making progress. This is particularly true if, as is often the case, the abuser has focused on the victim's mental weakness, frequently making remarks like, "You're crazy!" One must seek help and look after oneself not because of the abuser and what he says, but for oneself.

The psychotherapist Spiegel sums up the changes one should apply to traditional psychotherapy in order to adapt it for these victims: "In traditional psychotherapy one encourages the patient to assume greater responsibility for life's problems, whereas in these cases one must help the victim assume less responsibility for the traumatism."[3] Freeing themselves from guilt allows victims to regain their suffering, and it is only later, once the suffering has faded and they have healed, that they can look back at their history and try to understand why they entered into this type of destructive relationship and why they weren't able to defend themselves. One must live to be able to answer these questions.

A therapy focused only on the inner psyche encourages the victim to wallow in a state of depression and guilt and over-examine the circumstances, making her feel even more responsible for a process that involves two individuals. The danger lies in only looking at a possible trauma in her personal history, which would yield a linear and causal explanation for her suffering and would make the person responsible for her present unhappiness. Nonetheless, certain psychoanalysts not only refuse to pass moral judgment on the conduct or actions of the abusers who come to them for treatment, even when they are manifestly harmful to another individual; they will also deny the significance of the traumatism to the victim or make ironic remarks about the victim's tendency to dwell on the situation. Recently, psychoanalysts debating the subject of traumatism and its subjective effects showed how, ostensibly applying theory, they could humiliate the victim again, to subsequently make her answerable for her victimhood. In investigating the causes of failure and suffering, with references to masochism, they underlined the victim's irresponsibility when faced with what was killing her, as well as her delight in the role of victim. These same psychoanalysts questioned her innocence, arguing that there's a certain comfort derived from being a victim.

Even if certain points are valid, this reasoning is as mentally unhealthy as an abuser's outlook because there is no respect for the victim. There is no doubt that emotional abuse constitutes a trauma that results in suffering. As in any traumatism, the victim risks fixating on a particular aspect of her suffering, which prevents her from getting free of it. The conflict then takes over and dominates her thinking, especially if she hasn't been heard or understood and feels alone. Interpreting the obsession syndrome in terms of the victim's enjoyment only repeats, as one often sees, the traumatism. The wounds must first be bandaged before anything else is worked out and the victim can reactivate her thought processes.

How can a humiliated person confide in psychoanalysts who operate with admirable theoretical detachment but without empathy and kindness toward the victim?

FREEDOM FROM SUFFERING

A problem that one encounters in people who have been under the influence of some form of hidden violence or abuse is that they only seem to be able to function in one particular way and give the impression of being attached to their suffering. This syndrome is often interpreted by psychoanalysts as masochism. "Everything unfolds as if a foundation of suffering and abandonment had been unearthed by the analyst, which the patient considered his most precious gift, and without which he would be giving up his identity."[4] The tie with suffering relates to ties interwoven with others in a situation of suffering and pain. If ties or bonds are what make us human beings, it seems impossible for us to abandon them without separating ourselves from the people involved. One doesn't love suffering per se—that would constitute masochism—but one loves the whole context in which our first behaviors were learned.

It is dangerous to sensitize the patient too rapidly to her psychological dynamic, even when one knows that even if she got herself into a situation where she was controlled, there was in that situation a comforting element drawn from her childhood. The abuser intuitively was able to hook her because of a childhood fallibility. One can simply induce the patient into seeing the relationships between this most recent situation and her earlier wounds. This outcome can only be effected if one is certain she is free from under the abuser's hold and is sufficiently strong to assume her share of responsibility without becoming pathologically guilty.

Involuntary and unconscious memories repeat the traumatic situation. To avoid the anguish and suffering associated with memories of an experienced violence, the victims try to control their emotions but must learn to accept the pain, knowing it won't disappear right away, in order to begin living again. Through a real act of mourning, they must simultaneously let go of and accept their impotence. This will enable them to accept their deepest emotions and hurt and acknowledge their pain as a part of themselves worthy of respect. Only this acceptance will allow them to stop suffering and deluding themselves.

When victims begin to trust, they can relive the violence and their reactions to it, and reexamine the abusive situation and their role in it. They won't need to run from their memories and will be able to accept them in a new and different light.

HEALING

Healing means putting together again what has been blown to bits and re-establishing the ability to function. Therapy should allow the victim to realize that she cannot resume her role as victim. As she draws on her strength, the masochistic element in her that kept her controlled will give way on its own. For Paul Ricœur,[5] healing begins with memory and progresses through forgetfulness. According to him, too many memories cause suffering; one can be haunted by the remembrance of humiliations one has experienced or, on the contrary, suffer from a lack of memory and run away from one's past.

The patient must be brought to recognize her pain as a part of herself worthy of esteem, which will permit her to build a future. She must be brave enough to confront her wound.

The evolution of victims freed from another's ascendancy shows this is not a case of masochism, because very often their past painful experience teaches them a lesson: the victims learn to protect their autonomy, flee from verbal abuse, and refuse to accept any damage or injury to their self-esteem. Although the patient is not entirely masochistic, the abuser was able to wield his influence through an essential weakness that had masochistic tendencies. When an analyst tells a victim she relishes her suffering, he manages to eliminate the whole area of relationships. We are not isolated entities: we exist within a system of connections.

A traumatism experienced by an individual involves a restructuring of personality and a different relationship to the world. It leaves permanent traces upon which it is possible to rebuild. This wounding experience is often an opportunity for personal rebirth; one emerges stronger and less naïve and innocent. One decides that in the future, one will be respected. A human being who has been cruelly treated can draw new strength from a recognition of her past powerlessness. Ferenczi observes that extreme distress can suddenly awaken latent possibilities. The place within the individual kept void by the abuser attracts energy like a magnet: "Understanding doesn't simply spring from ordinary suffering, but only from traumatic suffering. It develops a secondary phenomenon or compensating factor to complete psychological paralysis."[5] "Abuser" then assumes a new meaning as a positive component in a life, allowing one to discover a previously repressed emotional knowledge and understanding.

PSYCHOTHERAPEUTIC OPTIONS

Choosing from among the numerous and diverse psychotherapies available is difficult. In France, psychoanalytical theory predominates, overshadowing other methods perhaps more ideally suited to take on immediate responsibility for the victims. Psychoanalysis has so widely and effectively imposed its body of knowledge on our culture that it has now become a common reference.

COGNITIVE-BEHAVIORAL PSYCHOTHERAPIES

The goal of cognitive-behavioral psychotherapies is to modify pathological symptoms and behaviors without acting on personality or its motivators.

The first intervention occurs at the level of stress. Through relaxation techniques, the patient learns to reduce physical tension, anxiety, and sleeping problems. Mastering these techniques is very useful in dealing with organizational abuse if the person attacked is still capable of defending herself. She can reduce the physical impact of stress by learning, for example, to control an angry outburst through relaxation and breathing exercises.

Another behavioral method consists in self-affirmation techniques. In the case of abuse victims, behavioral therapies[7] are based on the principle that victims are passive, non-affirming individuals lacking in self-confidence, as opposed to affirming subjects who clearly express their needs and refusals. This seems to me a very simplistic interpretation which leads one to believe that victims are habitually passive and non-affirming. We have already noted that although victims are generally scrupulous individuals with a tendency to want to over-achieve, in other contexts they have no trouble affirming themselves. A simplistic self-affirmation technique cannot unravel the complexities that allow an abuser to play his deadly game. Victims can, however, use these techniques to recognize manipulation, to understand that communication with an abuser is impossible, and to put less faith in their paradigms of ideal communication.

Behavioral therapies are sometimes coupled with cognitive   19⅂
therapies that teach the patient how to block out thoughts or
recurring images linked to the trauma; they can also teach
techniques to deal with present problems which, in the case of
abuse victims, would be learning how to counter-manipulate.

Cognitive restructuring seems a more interesting way to
help victims of abuse. Without being depressives, these individuals, as we have seen, have as part of their personalities a
predisposition toward depression, believing, for example, "If
I make a mistake, I am a worthless person." The abuser succeeds in gaining a hold on them through their basic principles:
devotion to others, a conscientious work ethic, and honesty.
The therapist can help the patients reach beyond the trauma
they have lived by lessening their feelings of guilt vis-à-vis
the trauma, by recognizing and supporting the anguish their
memories carry with them, and by acknowledging their past
impotence.

HYPNOSIS

Freud used hypnosis and the power of suggestion before abandoning them because they seemed to him based on seduction
and control. The practice of hypnosis has resurfaced in recent
years, particularly with the Ericksonian movement. Milton H.
Erickson has been designated an "out of the ordinary" therapist, although he never wrote down what he actually practiced.
He used hypnosis as well as other transformative strategies that
took into account the context in which the patient lived; this
gave him considerable influence on the development of systemic family therapy.

Techniques using hypnosis depend heavily on the capacity
for dissociation, which is highly developed in many victims of
trauma. François Roustang teaches that the fission created by

hypnosis resembles that brought about by trauma: it separates the bearable from the unbearable, which is relegated to the forgotten. These methods seek to help victims develop new perspectives that will diminish the suffering linked to trauma. It is not a case of awakening an awareness of psychological conflict, but a technique that will allow the patient to mobilize her own resources. The deeper the hypnosis, the more the person's individuality and resources become clear and she discovers a potential she'd never suspected she had.

This choice of method may appear contradictory. In hypnosis one must go through a stage of confusion in order to sever the symptoms; confusion was exactly what enabled the abusive control to be set in place. The therapist must use this confusion to allow the patient to reinvent her world by eliminating her inbred propensities for failure (which the abuser had previously used to impose his will and way of thinking), and transforming them. The choice of therapist is crucial when hypnosis is the methodology of choice; he or she must be extremely judicious and have great clinical experience. The patient must be wary of therapies that evoke traumatic memories without taking the whole individual into account.

SYSTEMIC PSYCHOTHERAPIES

Systemic family therapy does not concentrate on the symptomatic improvement of an individual; it focuses instead on communication and individuation of different members of the group. In couples therapy, the client is a couple and not one or the other partner; in family therapy, each member of the family is given equal attention and, in order to analyze an interactive process, the therapist abolishes any kind of labeling identification like "abuser" or "victim."

For systemic therapists, the word "victimology" may seem

like a return to linear interpretation. To recognize individual personality at the outset does not preclude taking into account its circular processes of reinforcement. One may cite the following example: An over-solicitous individual can aggravate in her partner a leaning toward dependency that the partner finds unbearable. The partner reacts in turn with rejection and aggressive behavior. The other, not understanding, feels responsible and becomes even more attentive, thereby intensifying her partner's rejection. This systemic explanation only makes sense if one considers the fact that one of these people is a narcissistic abuser and the other has a tendency to blame herself.

Systemic hypotheses such as the idea of homeostasis in families (maintaining equilibrium at any cost) or the idea of the double tie (blocking communication to paralyze the thought processes) help us understand how ascendancy or control establishes itself. However, on a purely clinical plane, severe systematic reasoning, which does not differentiate between abuser and abused and only recognizes a pathological relationship, risks losing sight of protecting the individual. Analyzing circular processes plays a useful role in diffusing an undeveloped situation: it permits the linkage of individual behaviors to that of other family members. Nevertheless, when abuse has graduated from the stage of control to that of outright harassment, the process takes on a life of its own; it is no longer possible to interrupt the process by depending on the players' logic and will to change.

Labeling abuse carries with it a moral connotation implying accusation and censure, which many therapists prefer to avoid. They prefer to discuss a perverse relationship in the abstract rather than naming an abuser and his victim. The abused person is then left abandoned to confront her guilt and is unable to free herself from the deadly abusive process. In any case, it is highly unlikely that a narcissistic abuser would ever agree to family or couples therapy because it's impossible for him to doubt himself. Individuals who dare to risk therapy can rely on abusive defense mechanisms without being true abusers. When therapeutic consultations are mandated by a judge, abusers tend to manipulate the mediator, trying to show just how bad his partner really is. It is very important, therefore, for therapists or mediators to remain on their guard against this strategy.

PSYCHOANALYSIS

Psychoanalytical therapy is not necessarily adapted to a victim still in shock from abusive violence and its attendant humiliations. Psychoanalysis focuses on "intrapsychology" without seriously considering pathologies induced by relationships with another person. Its goal is to analyze instinctive childhood conflicts that have been repressed. The rigid protocol prescribed by Freud to control transference (regular and frequent appointments, with the patient stretched out on a couch and the analyst out of sight) can lead to unbearable frustration in a person who has suffered from deliberately not being allowed to communicate, and might lead her to identify the psychoanalyst with the abuser, thereby perpetuating her state of dependence.

Only when the victim is sufficiently healthy should she undertake psychoanalysis to understand by remembering and working through what in her infancy and early childhood would explain her overly tolerant attitude toward the abuser; it would also help her to eliminate the weaknesses or faults that permitted the abusive control to take hold.

Whereas psychoanalysis aims to modify the underlying psychic structure, other psychotherapies seek symptomatic improvement and a reinforcement of defenses, which may also bring about deep psychological change. Either way, an initial healing phase is essential for a victim, who must disengage from what she has experienced most recently before evoking any childhood wounds.

Psychoanalysis alone won't work. No therapy can offer a miraculous solution that will spare the patient the work involved in change. The therapeutic framework is less important than the patient's commitment to the therapeutic methodology as well as a rigorous investment on the therapist's part. It is necessary for psychotherapists to become more open to other approaches and not limit themselves to one particular way of thinking. There are signs that more and more young psychiatrists and clinical psychologists are becoming sensitive to different psychoanalytical theories and are communicating amongst themselves. May we not foresee a bridge from one form of therapy to another, or even the integration of existing psychotherapeutic practices?

Throughout these pages, we have seen the unfolding of the abusive process in certain contexts. It seems clear, however, that the list is not definitive and that these circumstances reach beyond the worlds of the couple, the family, and the organization. They can be found in any kind of group where people compete: schools and universities, for example. Human imagination has no limits when it comes to destroying someone else's favorable self-image; in this way, we manage to cover up our own inherent weaknesses and assume a position of superiority. All of society is involved when power is involved. There have always been calculating, unscrupulous manipulators for whom the end justifies the means, but the proliferation of abusive acts in families and organizations points to the ascendancy of the individualism that dominates our society. In a system where the law of the strongest and the slyest reigns, abusers become kings. When success becomes the principal value, honesty looks weak and abuse seems resourceful.

Western societies, under the guise of tolerance, have gradually renounced their behavioral restraints and prohibitions. However, by too readily accepting what is wrong or harmful, as abused victims do, they develop abusive systems at the core. Numerous chief executives and politicians, potential role models for young people, are not overly concerned with morality when it comes to getting rid of a rival or staying in power. Some abuse their prerogatives, or use psychological pressure or so-called reasons of state to protect their private lives. Others get rich thanks to cunningly cutting corners in the area of social benefits, fiscal fraud, or general swindles. Corruption has become prevalent. Generally speaking, one or several abusive individuals in a group, an organization, or a government are enough to make the whole system abusive. If this abuse is not denounced, it spreads underground through intimidation, fear, and manipulation. To psychologically bind someone, influencing them to tell lies or compromise themselves will make them accomplices in the abusive process. It's the basic operational method of the Mafia and of most totalitarian regimes. Whether it be in families, organizations, or governments, narcissistic abusers arrange for others to take the blame for the disasters they themselves unleash in order to pose as saviors and thus seize positions of power; there, they can remain if they are unscrupulous. History has given us examples of human beings who refuse to recognize their mistakes, don't assume responsibility, tell lies, and manipulate reality to cover up traces of their wrong-doing.

Beyond the single question of emotional abuse, there are general questions we must ask ourselves. How do we reestablish respect between individuals? What should be the limits of tolerance? If individuals alone can't stop these destructive processes, society must intervene with legislation. Recently a projected law was filed against hazing, making it a misdemeanor, and repressing any degrading or humiliating act in an educational institution. If we do not want human relationships to be wholly regimented and governed by laws, we must make our children aware of the problem and educate them in order to prevent the continuation of emotionally abusive behavior.

AFTERWORD

BY THOMAS MOORE

One of the great mysteries is why human beings hurt each other physically and emotionally. Psychology has offered many explanations, but the phenomenon is still full of paradoxes.

Some writers who speak out for victims identify with those who apparently have no power, and I've heard of psychotherapists who encourage their clients to vent their anger and be as assertive as possible. It's difficult even for the observer—the family member, the friend, the professional—to avoid getting caught in the dizzying atmosphere of volatile emotions.

My own conclusion is that we are all made up of various degrees of strength and weakness, and indeed any human interaction involves subtle displays of dominance and submission. Power is a good thing, but it need not be dominating—exploiting others for narcissistic purposes. A person can have strength of personality without dominating others. Indeed, dominance suggests that there is little personal power present. A person can be vulnerable, too, without being submissive. Perhaps the best arrangement is a blend, never perfect, of strength and vulnerability.

Marie-France Hirigoyen raises many serious issues on these themes. Wisely, she recommends that we don't internalize and psychologize the whole problem, but recognize that life is full of extremes of the power problem. She also acknowledges that it is the soul that is wounded when power issues get out of hand.

201

This is a key point because real power in a person comes from a deep place, from the soul itself. It is not really personal, but rises up from that reservoir where our vitality is stored. In fact, personal power is almost indistinguishable from the life that is in us.

When parents, teachers, managers, police, and politicians try to repress the vitality of those in their charge, they are holding down the life force that threatens their desire to control. That repression is simultaneously an attack on the capacity in that person for personal strength. The result, as Ms. Hirigoyen points out, is turmoil and conflict. The soul is wounded and then expresses itself in a wounded manner. The delicate balance of strength and vulnerability within people and between them is lost, and abuse follows.

Ms. Hirigoyen recommends psychotherapy as one answer to these problems, and some form of professional intervention is certainly called for in cases where abuse is extreme. But I think we could also be educated to be more sophisticated about these issues. In most cases it appears that those in charge— those groups I mentioned—have never had a discussion or a class or direct guidance about the power issues in their various roles. They engage others with pure but devastating unconsciousness.

Acquiring deep personal strength is also part of the maturing process, where we discover that we don't have to purchase personal power at the expense of others. We may even find ways in which our own strength is nurtured.

To be personal for a moment: I am a reserved, shy person in most contexts, and I often give away too much of my own power. Yet my family tells me that I have an iron will and can be quite effective with my anger. I don't see these qualities in myself, but I'm sure my family is right. I will have to deal with my own power misalignments all my life. I never expect perfection, and although I have seen remarkable changes over the years, I'm quite sure the situation won't shift entirely.

As Ms. Hirigoyen points out, external sources of power and opportunities to be vulnerable are the key. I have found significant increases in personal strength simply from exercising my creativity. If I languish in my inactivity and worry, I just become more susceptible to the machinations of others who would like to control me. Although the issues involved are subtle and deeply interior, they certainly play themselves out in everyday life, and it is there that changes can take place.

We live in a violent world in which the abuse of power is usually rationalized and cleaned up. I think it would help to acknowledge exactly where we are strong and where we are weak, even as a nation. This need not be done in a self-mocking fashion but rather in a spirit of honesty and forthrightness. There is nothing wrong with having power and nothing wrong in being vulnerable. We could be exactly where we feel in these areas and then let the extremes find their middle ground by a natural alchemy rather than by force or program.

I might mention one further point about this problem. As we say in archetypal psychology, go with the symptom. If you seem to be abusive, don't try to be vulnerable. Try to be strong in more subtle and more creative ways. If you suffer too much and play the victim role, don't try to be assertive. Discover effective ways to be vulnerable.

We might also bring in the spiritual dimension. Ultimate vulnerability is the recognition that we can't control life. We can feel our personal power without exploiting it at anyone else's expense. This absolute surrender to life is the beginning of a spiritual attitude, and, I believe, the best solution to the problem of abuse.

NOTES

CHAPTER ONE

1. J. G. Lemaire, *Le couple: sa vie, sa mort* (Paris: Payot, 1979).

2. A. Miller, *For Your Own Good: Hidden Cruelty in Child-rearing and the Roots of Violence*, trans. Hildegarde and Hunter Hannum (New York: Farrar, Straus & Giroux, 1990).

3. S. Ferenczi, "Confusion de langue entre les adultes et l'enfant," in *Psychanalyse IV* (Paris: Payot, 1985).

4. B. Lempert, *Désamour* (Paris: Le Seuil, 1989).

5. B. Lempert, *L'enfant et le désamour* (Éditions L'Arbre au milieu, Paris, 1989).

6. A. Miller, *The Untouched Key: Tracing Childhood Trauma in Creativity and Destructiveness*, trans. Hildegarde and Hunter Hannum (New York: Doubleday, 1991).

7. P. C. Racamier, *L'inceste et l'incestuel* (Paris: Les Éditions du Collège, 1995).

CHAPTER TWO

1. H. Leymann, *Mobbing* (Paris: Le Seuil, 1996).

2. Fitzgerald, "Sexual Harassment: The Definition and Measurement of a Construct," in *Ivory Power: Sexual Harassment on Campus*, ed. M. A. Paludi (Albany: State University of New York Press, 1990).

3. MacKinney and Maroules (1991), cited by G. F. Pinard in *Criminalité et psychiatrie* (Paris: Ellipses, 1997).

4. S. Milgram, *Obedience to Authority* (New York: HarperCollins, 1983).

5. C. Dejours, *Souffrance en France* (Paris: Le Seuil, 1998).

6. N. Aubert and V. de Gaulejac, *Le coût de l'excellence* (Paris: Le Seuil, 1991).

CHAPTER THREE

1. P. C. Racamier, "Pensée perverse et décervelage," in *Secrets de famille et pensée perverse, Gruppo* no. 8 (Paris: Éditions Apsygée, 1992).

2. J. Baudrillard, *Seduction*, trans. Brian Singer (New York: St. Martin's Press, 1990).

3. *Diagnostic and Statistical Manual of Mental Disorders*, 4th ed. (*DSM-IV*) (Washington, D.C.: American Psychiatric Association, 1994).

4. R. Dorey, "La relation d'emprise," in *Nouvelle revue de psychanalyse*, no. 24 (Paris: Gallimard, 1981).

CHAPTER FOUR

1. Sun Tsu, *The Art of War*, ed. and with a foreword by James Clavell (New York: Delacorte Press, 1989).

2. *Le Monde*, 18 November 1996.

CHAPTER FIVE

1. M. Hurni and G. Stoll, *La haine de l'amour (La perversion du lien)*, (Paris: L'Harmattan, 1996).

2. R. Perrone and M. Nannini, *Violence et abus sexuels dans la famille* (Paris: ESF, 1995).

CHAPTER SIX

1. J. Laplanche and J. B. Pontalis, *The Language of Psychoanalysis* (New York: W. W. Norton, 1973).

2. J. Bergeret, *La personnalité normale et pathologique* (Paris: Bordas, 1985).

3. P. C. Racamier, "Pensée perverse et décervelage," in *Secrets de famille et pensée perverse, Gruppo* no. 8 (Paris: Éditions Apsygée, 1992).

4. A. Eiguer, *Le pervers narcissique et son complice* (Paris: Dunod, 1996).

5. O. Kernberg, "The Narcissistic Personality," in *Borderline Conditions and Pathological Narcissism* (New York: Jason Aronson, 1975).

6. Ovid, *The Metamorphoses*, trans. Mary Annes (New York: Viking Press, 1987).

1. R. Girard, *Violence and the Sacred,* trans. Patrick Gregory (Baltimore: Johns Hopkins University Press, 1979).

2. S. Freud, "The Economic Problem of Masochism," in *The Standard Edition of the Complete Psychological Works of Sigmund Freud,* trans. and ed. James Strachey (London: Hogarth Press, 1957).

3. F. Roustang, *How to Make a Paranoid Laugh: Or What Is Psychoanalysis?* (Philadelphia: University of Pennsylvania Press, 2000).

4. F. Kafka, *The Trial,* trans. George Steiner (New York: Knopf, 1992).

5. H. Tellenbach, *Melancholy: History of the Problem, Endogeneity, Typology, Pathogenesis, Clinical Considerations* (Pittsburgh: Duquesne University Press, 1980).

6. B. Cyrulnik, *Sous le signe du lien* (Paris: Hachette, 1989).

7. M. Khan, *Alienation in Perversions* (New York: International Universities Press, 1979).

8. A. Miller, *The Drama of the Gifted Child,* trans. Ruth Ward (New York: HarperCollins, 1996).

CHAPTER NINE

1. C. Classen, C. Koopman, and D. Siegel, "Trauma and Dissociation," *Bulletin of the Menninger Clinic* 57, no. 2 (1993).

2. *Diagnostic and Statistical Manual of Mental Disorders,* 4th ed. (*DSM-IV*) (Washington, D.C.: American Psychiatric Association, 1994).

3. S. Ferenczi, "Psychanalyse des névroses de guerre (1918)," in *Psychanalyse III* (Paris: Payot, 1990).

4. M. A. Dutton and L. Goodman, "Post-traumatic Stress Disorder Among Battered Women: Analysis of Legal Implications," in *Behavioral Sciences and the Law* 12 (1994): 215–234.

5. L. Crocq, "Les victimes psychiques," in *Victimologie* (November 1994).

CHAPTER ELEVEN

1. The requirements of this law are rigorous and difficult to satisfy. Liability can only be found when the defendant's conduct has

been "extreme" and "outrageous." It has not been enough that the defendant has acted with an intent that is tortious or even criminal, or that he has intended to inflict emotional distress, or even that his conduct has been characterized by "malice," or a degree of aggravation that would entitle the plaintiff to punitive damages for another tort. To date, every one of these claims has failed in New York state courts because the alleged conduct was not considered to be sufficiently outrageous.

CHAPTER TWELVE

1. S. Ferenczi, "Confusion de langue entre les adultes et l'enfant," in *Psychanalyse IV* (Paris: Payot, 1985).

2. C. Damiani, *Les victimes* (Paris: Bayard Éditions, 1997).

3. D. Spiegel, "Dissociation and Hypnosis in Post-Traumatic Stress Disorders," in *Journal of Traumatic Stress* 1: 17–33.

4. F. Roustang, *How to Make a Paranoid Laugh: Or What is Psychoanalysis?* (Philadelphia: University of Pennsylvania Press, 2000).

5. P. Ricœur, "Le pardon peut-il guérir?" *Esprit*, March–April 1995.

6. S. Ferenczi, *Psychanalyse IV,* op. cit.

7. I. Nazare-Aga, *Les manipulateurs sont parmi nous* (Ivry: Les éditions de l'homme, 1997).

8. A. Miller, *The Untouched Key: Tracing Childhood Trauma in Creativity and Destructiveness*, trans. Hildegarde and Hunter Hannum (New York: Doubleday, 1991).

BIBLIOGRAPHY

Aubert, N., and V. de Gaulejac. *Le coût de l'excellence.* Paris: Le Seuil, 1991.

Baudrillard, J. *Seduction.* Translated by Brian Singer. New York: St. Martin's Press, 1990.

Bergeret, J. *La personnalité normale et pathologique.* Paris: Bordas, 1985.

Classen, C., C. Koopman, and D. Siegel. "Trauma and Dissociation." *Bulletin of the Menninger Clinic* 57, no. 2 (1993).

Crocq, L. "Les victimes psychiques." *Victimologie* (November 1994).

Cyrulnik, B. *Sous le signe du lien.* Paris: Hachette, 1989.

Damiani, C. *Les victimes.* Paris: Bayard Éditions, 1997.

Dejours, C. *Souffrance en France.* Paris: Le Seuil, 1998.

Diagnostic and Statistical Manual of Mental Disorders, 4th ed. (*DSM-IV*) Washington, D.C.: American Psychiatric Association, 1994.

Dorey, R. "La relation d'emprise." *Nouvelle revue de psychanalyse,* no. 24. Paris: Gallimard, 1981.

Dutton, M. A., and L. Goodman. "Post-traumatic Stress Disorder Among Battered Women: Analysis of Legal Implications." *Behavioral Sciences and the Law* 12 (1994): 215–234.

Eiguer, A. *Le pervers narcissique et son complice.* Paris: Dunod, 1996.

Ferenczi, S. "Confusion de langue entre les adultes et l'enfant (1932)." *Psychanalyse IV.* Paris: Payot pour la traduction française, 1985.

Ferenczi, S. "Psychanalyse des névroses de guerre (1918)." *Psychanalyse III.* Paris: Payot pour la traduction française, 1990.

Ferenczi, S. "The Development of Psycho-Analysis." *Classics in Psychoanalysis, Monograph 4.* New York: International Universities Press, 1986.

Fitzgerald. "Sexual Harassment: The Definition and Measurement of a Construct." *Ivory Power: Sexual Harassment on Campus.* Edited by M. A. Paludi. Albany: State University of New York Press, 1990.

209

210   Freud, S. "The Economic Problem of Masochism." *The Standard Edition of the Complete Psychological Works of Sigmund Freud.* Translated and edited by James Strachey. London: Hogarth Press, 1957.

Girard, R. *Violence and the Sacred.* Translated by Patrick Gregory. Baltimore: Johns Hopkins University Press, 1979.

Hurni, M., and G. Stoll. *La haine de l'amour (La perversion du lien).* Paris: L'Harmattan, 1996.

Kafka, F. *The Trial.* Translated by George Steiner. New York: Knopf, 1992.

Kernberg, O. "The Narcissistic Personality." *Borderline Conditions and Pathological Narcissism.* New York: Jason Aronson, 1975.

Khan, M. Masud R. *Alienation in Perversions.* New York: International Universities Press, 1979.

Laplanche, J., and J. B. Pontalis. *The Language of Psychoanalysis.* New York: W. W. Norton, 1973.

Lemaire, J. G. *Le couple: sa vie, sa mort.* Paris: Payot, 1979.

Lempert, B. *Désamour.* Paris: Le Seuil, 1989.

Lempert, B. *L'enfant et le désamour.* Paris: Éditions l'Arbre au milieu, 1989.

Leymann, H. *Mobbing.* Paris: Le Seuil pour la traduction française, 1996.

MacKinney and Maroules (1991), cited by G. F. Pinard. *Criminalité et psychiatrie.* Paris: Ellipses, 1997.

Milgram, S. *Obedience to Authority.* New York: HarperCollins, 1983.

Miller, A. *The Drama of the Gifted Child.* Translated by Ruth Ward. New York: HarperCollins, 1996.

Miller, A. *For Your Own Good: Hidden Cruelty in Child-rearing and the Roots of Violence.* Translated by Hildegarde and Hunter Hannum. New York: Farrar, Straus & Giroux, 1990.

Miller, A. *The Untouched Key: Tracing Childhood Trauma in Creativity and Destructiveness.* Translated by Hildegarde and Hunter Hannum. New York: Doubleday, 1991.

Nazare-Aga, I. *Les manipulateurs sont parmi nous.* Ivry: Les éditions de l'homme, 1997.

Ovid, *The Metamorphoses.* Translated by Mary Annes. New York: Viking Press, 1987.

Perrone, R., and M. Nannini. *Violence et abus sexuels dans la famille.* Paris: ESF, 1995.

Racamier, P. C. *L'inceste et l'incestuel.* Paris: Les Éditions du Collège, 1995.

Racamier, P. C. "Pensée perverse et décervelage." *Secrets de famille et pensée perverse, Gruppo* no. 8. Paris: Éditions Apsygée, 1992.

Ricœur, P. "Le pardon peut-il guérir?" *Esprit,* March–April, 1995.

Roustang, F. *How to Make a Paranoid Laugh: Or What Is Psychoanalysis?* Philadelphia: University of Pennsylvania Press, 2000.

Spiegel, D. "Dissociation and Hypnosis in Post-Traumatic Stress Disorders." *Journal of Traumatic Stress* 1: 17–33.

Tellenbach, H. *Melancholy: History of the Problem, Endogeneity, Typology, Pathogenesis, Clinical Considerations.* Pittsburgh: Duquesne University Press, 1980.

Tsu, Sun. *The Art of War.* Edited and with a foreword by James Clavell. New York: Delacorte Press, 1989.